The Missing List

a memoir

Clare Best

Published by Linen Press, London 2018
8 Maltings Lodge
Corney Reach Way
London
W4 2TT
www.linen-press.com

A CIP catalogue record for this book is available from the British Library.

Cover art: Neil Gower
Author photograph: Derek Adams
Typeset by Zebedee Design, Edinburgh
Printed and bound by Lightning Source

ISBN 9781999604615

About the author

 Clare Best decided when she was six that she wanted to be a writer. Along the way she has worked as a fine bookbinder, a bookseller and an editor. She writes poetry as well as prose and often collaborates with visual artists. Clare has presented her acclaimed autobiographical project *Self-portrait without Breasts* across the UK and Ireland and in the USA and Canada. She has held writing residencies in settings as various as Woodlands Organic Farm, HMP Shepton Mallet and the University of Brighton. Her work has won prizes, Arts Council England awards and an Authors' Foundation grant from the Society of Authors. She lives near the Suffolk coast with her husband and their whippet.

Other books by Clare Best:

Treasure Ground

Excisions

Breastless

CELL

Springlines

for all the children
and for Mica

in memory of my mother
Heather Best (née Gardner)

Foreword

My parents met on a blind date in London, towards the end of
the Second World War, when those who were young and single
were hurrying to find a partner and settle down before the music
stopped.

My mother always said she fell in love with my father's voice
when he telephoned to arrange to collect her for his stepsister's
wedding party. My father maintained he fell in love with my
mother's scent while they sat together in the taxi through the
blackout of a wartime London night. A blind date, indeed. They
married a year or two later when my father was demobbed from
the Navy.

My father was born into a family of the minor aristocracy
and his father was connected to the tea trade in India. Although
he was materially privileged, my father's childhood and youth
were not happy. His mother died when he was five. He was sent
to boarding school less than two years later when his father
married again, this time to the archetypal wicked stepmother.
She moved her own children into the best rooms, sent my father
and his siblings to stand by their mother's grave when they were
disobedient, and squandered her new husband's money. All his
life my father had an irreconcilable double perception of the
opposite sex: woman as perfect and unattainable (his mother)

and woman as wicked and ever-present (his stepmother). Neither version was to be trusted.

The blithe and pretty auburn-haired girl who became my mother was the younger of two daughters from an upper middle class professional family. She was quick-witted but left school early to be a Red Cross nurse in Chelsea during the Blitz. She played as hard as she worked. Her War was a whirl of dances with handsome, hard-drinking servicemen, each of whom – according to the stories she later told me – wanted to marry her and whisk her away to a distant part of the world when the War was over. The love of her life, a gallant RAF pilot, went missing over France in 1944. She was heartbroken. Some five months later, that black Bakelite telephone rang in her parents' flat in Queensgate Gardens and she picked it up. The scene was set.

Starting in 1948, my parents had five children, a typical post-war baby-boomer family. Their second son died as a toddler. There were other ghosts and there were layers of secrets, on both sides. My father was a particularly complex character, full of contradictions and unexplored anger. He was authoritarian and, within our family, a cruel bully.

The family became an echo chamber for events and feelings my parents could not confront. As the fourth child of five, and the only girl, my role was not just the traditional one of carer. I was the aerial, the listening device, the lightning conductor or, as one of my brothers put it, the sacrificial anode. Later, I became the interpreter, the speaker.

The way I've written this story does not form a narrative in any conventional sense. My collection of offcuts is more like a collage, but this reflects my experience. One source is a journal I kept throughout the year leading up to my father's death. There

8

are tape recordings from the same period of my father talking about his life. I've included passages of my own reflective writing based on my memories. And I describe family scenes from Bolex ciné-film footage taken by my father.

Nine years after my father's death, I'm beginning to appreciate how I experienced these years, and the years leading up to his death, as a powerful vortex. I'm thankful that I've been able to keep working on this book throughout this period, although sometimes I've set it aside for months or years at a time. Even when the work has consumed energy I felt I couldn't spare, it has always helped me to process and cope with what happened to me.

As time passed, this writing found several aims. The first was to articulate at last my childhood truth and its legacy. The second was to reclaim what little I could of my relationship with my father. In achieving those, I understood and realised a third, vitally important aim which was to find a satisfactory way of rendering in words something of my fragmented emotional life.

The subject of child abuse in all its many forms is crowded with taboos of which the taboo surrounding sexual abuse of a child by a parent must be the most persistent, disturbing and mysterious. We don't understand why children are harmed in this way nor do we know how to think and talk about it. We do know that the wounds and pain are often invisible and long-lasting and that this damage wrecks lives, causing physical, emotional and mental distress, illness and death.

Whilst the work I've done with my memories has been intensely personal, I hope that publishing this book might help to bring light into one of the darkest areas of human suffering.

I am one of the lucky ones. I made it through. There are too many who do not – our prisons, hospitals and cemeteries are full of them. And so I give you my story, hoping it may help to break down myths and misunderstandings around abuse and its aftermath.

My father was and is the only father I can ever have. It is painful to know that I'll always think of him with fear in my heart, along with a mixture of feelings that I call love and hate because I don't know how else to name them. Feeling these emotions and many more has enabled me to survive, and continuing to tune in to them may be necessary for my sanity. It is a strange paradox that being able to know and tolerate emotional extremes is what heals the split in me.

This book began as an act of compassion for my young self. It became a way of trying to understand and accept my father. I can see now that when I started writing the book, in patches between 2003 and 2006, I was still in thrall to my father. I was protecting him and searching for explanations for what he did. It was an illusion that I was becoming free of him. I realise that I might never be completely free of him but finally I know the complexities of his behaviour. I see him for what he was. In that sense I *am* free. In that sense, it is the right time to publish.

I've wrestled with the idea of acceptance, never mind forgiveness, as the long-term effects of the abuse have become more evident to me. Seeing the impact more clearly, I judge my father more fairly. Today I feel more kindness towards myself and less towards the adult who must have known precisely what he was doing. It has been interesting to observe this shift.

I have been in therapy for many years, a journey that has run in parallel to my writing. Both have helped me to find my lost self as well as to express grief for the loving relationship my father and I should have had, and didn't.

Making this book has been a strange kind of salvage operation. It tells my individual truth: the testament of one witness to the immense confusion and suffering that an abusive human being can cause. It's also part of a broader truth shared by others who have had to live through something similar. It's very real, though it hasn't always felt real. It's quicksilver; it's lead. Writing it has been the best I could do. It has also been the most difficult thing I've ever done.

Suffolk, September 2018

Author's notes

The sections in my father's voice have been transcribed word for word from recordings we made together when he was telling the story of his life. Some people's names have been altered. Names of family houses remain unchanged and a timeline of these homes can be found below.

This memoir holds something of my own story, and parts of my father's and my mother's. It does not attempt to tell the story of the family as a whole and it cannot tell the stories of other family members. My brothers' experiences have been different from mine and their narratives are their own. By deliberately including only light sketches of them in scenes from long ago, I have respected their privacy. I have mostly left out references to them during the later stages of my father's life. Although each played a part in helping to meet my father's needs when he was ill and dying, my experience of caring for my father at that time was intensely solitary and it remains so in memory.

My husband Philip has been with me on my journey, and has helped me adjust to each discovery and revelation from my early life. He has known when to protect me and when to let me do what I needed to do. Our son, Freddie, has been a constant source of joy and pride.

Some of the family homes:

Pathfields, Exmouth	1951–1954
Bracknell, Dartford	1954–1958
Broomfields, Dartford	1958–1962
My grandmother's house at Richmond Avenue, Bexhill	1961–1964
Manor Farm, Sussex	1962–1973
Meadow Court, Wiltshire	1973–1976
Monks House, Hampshire	1976–1997
Forest Brow Care Home (my mother)	1996–1999
Ridgeway (my father)	1997–2009

28 August, 2008

I wake in the night to the hypnotic sound of rain falling on water. A storm over Lake Maggiore. Metallic sheets of lightning rattle overhead. The tablecloth flaps on my balcony table. And there's the lap, lap, lap of high lake water.

I can't sleep. Towards dawn I pull back the curtains to sit at the open window. By seven, high cirrus clouds are all that's left of the wild night. Green runs over the landscape like a fever, painting palm trees, islands and forested hills. The rest is water and sky.

I can smell caramel, coffee and the scent of moisture drawn from wood by the sun.

Shutters are banging open. Doormats are being beaten.

The first poplar and beech leaves are blowing onto the lake's surface today, crisp and colourful on the black. This morning I will swim again in the blood-warm water. It is my ink.

Tonight I must go home to England. Back to Dad and his long dying.

I write because it's better than not writing. I write with my ink on his paper.

* * *

I was once a six-year-old with long blonde hair. My eyes were the colour of the English Channel, or so my mother liked to tell me.

Each morning I'd sit on her knee in the kitchen while she brushed my hair until it crackled with static.

She used to say I'd been given the wrong pair of ears. *They're too big for you.* I loved the way she laughed when she said that, her eyes creased at the corners.

* * *

I give thanks that my father lifted me up so I could peer into the vats of bubbling pulp.

I give thanks for the paper rolling on felts over the machines, for those huge metal cylinders, hot and smooth and dangerous, for the long tubes of bright light high above my head.

I give thanks for the different coloured papers, for being given samples to take home.

They are good memories, these titbit recollections of visits to Dartford paper mill on Saturday afternoons.

* * *

At work, my father made paper. At home he made films.

After tea on Sundays, after he'd poured a large gin and tonic and shut himself in his study, I'd take up my vigil outside his door. Kneeling on the floorboards in the hall and stretching up towards the keyhole, I would press my left ear to its cold brass surround. I closed my eyes to make myself invisible and listened with every part of me. Even as a seven-year-old, I was patient and determined.

The noises were faint and muffled. Some were always the same. I had worked them out: a series of rattles as he rolled down the blackout blinds; a thud as he put a box on his desk; another thud as he lowered a box to the floor. The clank of tins and lids. A few minutes later, a whirring that started and stopped. Rapid clicking: a machine being wound up. Then that repeated swift rasping sound like paper being slit.

And his voice. *Ah, here's the one I'm after. Gently does it. Damn thing. Why won't it stick? Shit. Bugger... BUGGER.*

Week after week I knelt outside the door and listened as he cut and spliced.

Sometimes I'd go and pick scraps of celluloid out of his wastepaper basket the next day and hold them up to the light. A tiny blurry face or a patch of darkness. Almost nothing at all.

* * *

Ciné film, 1955
A lone Scots piper in the foreground, standing on an arched stone bridge in a forest. Zoom in: knee-length socks with garters, kilt and sporran, double-breasted black jacket. The piper waves to someone beyond camera to his right, then resumes blowing. Cut to waterfall. Peaty water bubbling over dark rocks. Cascades speeded up, double time. Now to sombre hillsides and a quick panning shot across a murky horizon. Stony outcrops and heather. Acres of good luck. Suddenly someone moves into the right of the frame, walking two steps sideways. The girl's mother. And someone else. The mother's mother. They stand side by side for two or three seconds, both leaning back against what must be a car because chrome trim is just visible, then a number plate and windscreen wipers. The younger woman is looking down, left hand on her belly. She is heavily pregnant. As she turns, the bump is silhouetted briefly against stormy mountains behind. Then the figures are gone. The film quality fails now. Invasions

of reds and yellows. At last the laddered squares of black. The
end of a reel.

* * *

We have this in common, my father and I – our cutting rooms. First, I write. In that writing, I find out who I am, what I think. Later I decide what to keep, what to toss in the bin. Here I am now, splicing my own life together.

I was born in Dartford, in my parents' bedroom, on a humid July night two weeks past my due date. My father had bought flowers for my mother a full seven days before I arrived, because he was going away on a business trip. He put them in the fridge to keep them fresh.

The flowers turned into slimy compost and I was not a beautiful baby. My skin was dry and flaky and my right eye swollen as though I'd been in a fight. Later, when I began to look around me, the right eye didn't move in tandem with the left.

All through my childhood, my mother watched out for the wandering eye. *Bring your eye in*, she'd say and only then did I realise I'd drifted into a split world. A place where everything was both solid and ghostly, side by side.

* * *

12 September, 2008
The doctors no longer make predictions for Dad. They say the cancer is unstoppable. It began as prostate cancer, and although it was slow for a while and was kept in check with drugs, now it's on the move.

All life is borrowed time. Dad's time is loaned on a short term and at a high rate of interest.

Things shift in and out of focus. In this interval between his life and his death, I'm laying out the bits of the puzzle and seeing how they might fit together. The intensity of it terrifies me but the terror carries me along. There is, of course, a deadline, though I can't know when it will come. Months, or weeks.

I want to use the time that's left. I want to make some kind of sense of our relationship. And I need to achieve a state of mind that will bear his leaving.

I want to understand. I think I'm just about ready.

* * *

I've discovered a bubble in the window of my study at the top of the house, a flaw in the old glass about three inches in diameter. The bubble works like a magnifying glass. If I look through it in a certain way I can recreate my youthful double vision. I can split things in two.

When I stand at the window and gaze out over the town, as I do when I'm thinking, I can move that bubble lens across roofs and gardens, clouds and chimney pots. I pick out one branch on a beech tree, its leaves curling. I slice bark off a trunk or divide a telegraph pole, keeping the curved line in suspense, away from the original surface. I can let it settle back there when I want, just by the way I look through the bubble.

If my subject is moving, I move my head to keep it in my sights. I follow the flight of a gull or a dove, and then I hold the bird just so at the edge of the lens, divide it, clone it.

I make two birds, and watch them fly in parallel for as long as I choose.

And now I examine a loose tile on the side of my neighbour's house. I home in on the open window next to it, the shadows shifting inside the room. A figure comes to the casement, looks down on the street. I trap his pale torso under my lens and I split him.

* * *

14 September, 2008
There's a memory Dad likes to think of now, at the end of his life. I've heard him mention it so many times. He always begins like this:

Do you remember how we used to go and hide away under that cliff in Cornwall? Nobody knew we were there, nobody could see us.

Yes, I tell him. *I remember.*

But I'm not sure I do.

* * *

Write what you know, some say. Some say write what you don't know. I say write what you need to know. Write what you have to remember, what you want to forget.

When did all of this begin, this need to make sense of who I am, this drive to reclaim myself? Was it when my mother was recovering from breast cancer and, aged sixteen, I sat on her bed and listened to the story of her life, and her version of my father's?

Was it years later, after her death in 1999, when I retreated to an armchair with the big blue scrapbook she kept throughout my childhood, and studied the loops and misspellings of her handwritten account of my early years?

Perhaps it began in earnest during my later obsessive viewing of those old family ciné films until I knew every mote of dust, every clumsy edit?

I don't think it much matters where or when it began. There's a series of beginnings. A habit. I begin and begin. I search, desperate to find out more about why I feel incomplete but unable to read the blanks and the blankness. I only know that something vital has been lost, and without it I can't find out what else is missing.

Another day of readiness, when the only way to start is to place something on the page. I don't know if I can trust myself to tell the story as it should be told, as far as it can be told. But I am writing this and you are reading it. That is a beginning.

* * *

Ciné film, 1956
The girl toddles to camera in tight baby breeches with spats over tiny blue leather Start-Rite shoes. A pink woollen overcoat sticks out over her prosperous tummy. Her head is spherical in a white felt hat with bobble and chinstrap. She's about eighteen months old. The slow staggering is guided by a headless adult at her side. The woman's pleated skirt brushes against her shoes when she leans forward to steady the girl. Now, suddenly, a glimpse of the top of the woman's head, dark permed waves. A change. A different bit of footage. The girl is a few weeks more confident. This time a small boy with reddish hair holds her right hand, the woman still has her left. The girl is pulling ahead on rigid legs

until finally she lets go of both the helping hands and topples forwards across an area of snow-patched flagstones. The woman stoops to pick her up. Then she relinks the small gloved hand with the boy's. Two children, propped together. Companions because of genes and timing. The girl's face is pink and tear-stained while her brother smiles and jiggles his eyebrows for the camera. The woman plants a teddy bear in the girl's arms. The boy slips his hand from his sister's, twists one of his ankles behind and around the other until his feet are on the ground, right for left and left for right, and silly-walks off.

* * *

5 *October, 2008*

Dad's birthday. When I called him this morning, he told me he wants to write the story of his life.

Setting things down is a duty, he says.

He wants to make a record because it's important that his four children and six grandchildren know a bit about him. He wants to do this before it's too late.

He wants his account to be *objective,* he tells me. He goes on, *I can't abide slurs on relationships. I want to tell the truth but perhaps that won't always be appropriate.*

* * *

My mother's kitchen is a place in my head, a blend, a confection of all her kitchens and mine. And this place where we meet, the small child self and I, is something like my mother's kitchen.

The first kitchen I can recall is at Broomfields, in Dartford.

The room is dark at all times of day with small windows of leaded lights and a deep-red lino floor. To me, it's a theatre where shows are put on. There's a cast-iron range and, near it, an all-enveloping Parker Knoll armchair patterned with large exotic flowers.

A few steps away is the enormous porcelain sink in which I am bathed each evening after tea. A pink child quietly surveying the steam and the predictable activity of early evening, I'm another pot to be soaked and scrubbed. Later I'm sat on the wooden-slatted draining board, where I wait to be dried.

In this kitchen, I'm still four years old. I spend most of my time close to the floor, and the daylight or electric light is somewhere near my feet, flooding under doors in strange angular shapes. It seems I'll never be big enough to touch the twisty black metal window fittings or fetch a soup bowl from the top shelf of the white-painted dresser.

My mother comes and goes from the store cupboard which is stashed with condensed milk, Spam, rice, Marmite, Heinz Cream of Tomato Soup, boxes of Fruit Jellies, porridge oats. Sometimes I sit on the window seat in the draughty alcove where we eat our family meals, and watch her cooking. She's wearing a cotton apron over a full cotton skirt and slow-dancing around the kitchen in a pattern which, if I study it for long enough, begins to make sense. She shares secrets about melting butter and sieving flour. In due time, I learn to break eggs. She lets me help her stir.

My grandmother's last kitchen is part of my mother's kitchen too. This room is by the sea. It tastes of salt, town gas and toast. I mustn't go near the cooker with its four open flames like sentinels, and its flashing blue-and-orange gas grill that simultaneously shrinks and browns the slices of white bread.

I relax in my grandmother's ample lap while she sits at the table shucking peas. When the toast is ready for turning, she sets me down and I wait solemnly for her to come back.

Another kitchen: this time at Manor Farm, in the High Weald of Sussex. I'm seven when my parents buy the house. This kitchen is the only one my mother designs herself. A fitted kitchen, with light-wood Ercol furniture. In winter, robins come in through the open window by the stainless-steel sink. They hop nervously into our domain, eat the Atora suet my mother leaves on the sill for them, and bounce away again.

Beyond that window, in the sheltered corner of the yard outside, my father has built an aviary to house my mother's budgerigars – blues, canary yellows and greens, lavenders, whites and subtle peaches. There must be thirty of them at the peak of her collecting years. She and I watch them feed while we do the washing up on a Sunday afternoon as the sun goes down behind Brightling Beacon. I'm tall enough now to see clouds and hills over the sink. I'm almost as tall as my mother.

In this kitchen, a few years later, I wear my mother's apron and learn to follow her recipes and clean her pans on my own. I feed her family. I reproduce her Saturday mince with tomatoes and her chocolate cake with Cadbury's Dairy Milk melted over the top. She's upstairs in bed, newly home from hospital. Breast cancer, a radical mastectomy, though I won't know that for months.

* * *

18 October, 2008

Another exchange about Dad's memoir. It's his idea that I'll *take dictation* – write down his words with a pen on sheets of lined paper. My idea is that I'll sit with him and let him speak with a tape recorder running. After some hesitation, he reluctantly accepts my version.

To prepare, I suggest he jots down a few important dates from his life and sketches out a basic timeline with key events, people, themes, specific memories and anecdotes. These will act as prompts while we sit and talk. Sometimes I'll ask questions to encourage him to elaborate.

He finds this plan helpful. He's agreed to think about the material and we've made a first date to meet at his house. As usual, I'm expected to go over there. He's made the seventy-minute journey to visit me and Philip and Freddie only four or five times in the almost ten years we've lived here.

In some odd way I feel flattered that he's asked me to help with this project. Is it his way of acknowledging, finally, that I'm a writer? But I also feel anxious about seeing him. That hasn't changed. Our meetings usually consist of a stiff and awkward lunch. At least this time there'll be a focus.

* * *

Ciné film, 1957
Bracknell, Dartford. A garden full of gaudy flowers, bicycles,
several children. Zoom in on a stone birdbath and a paddling pool
next to it where the girl, now a confident toddler, is splashing her
red-haired brother. He splashes her back. Cut to a family group
in the same garden. Rare posed footage, almost a still. The
children's mother is sitting centre shot. She has her right arm
around the tallest boy who leans away from her, reaching out to
stroke the dog, a Rhodesian Ridgeback. The woman's left arm

25

encircles the red-haired boy and the girl. They stand looking at camera, barely moving except for occasional mute utterances. The woman smiles, tilts her head to the left, and squints. The girl does likewise. The red-haired boy and the tall thin boy stick their tongues out.

* * *

29 October, 2008

The day has come. I'm strangely excited.

Dad and I have never sat down together to work on something I love doing. We've climbed up and skied down the same mountains but in our different ways. We've sat at the same table, eating and drinking, possibly for months if you added up all the hours and yet we might as well have been sitting at separate tables. And the night after I took my mother to Forest Brow Care Home, Dad and I both got drunk in her kitchen. I cried and his eyes filled with tears, and we stood like this at each end of the counter, unable to share our independent griefs.

But we've never embarked on any true exchange of ideas, and managed to meet halfway. This project is the closest we've ever come to collaboration. Of course it's still on his terms because he's in charge and I am most definitely the child. It's rather like, in the old days, being admitted to his study for an audience.

For each of us this enterprise is fraught with risk but for me it feels like skydiving from a plane that's on fire. Add to this that I've never had any skydiving training, and I've been told the parachute hasn't been checked. I feel compelled to jump even though I've no idea how it will all end.

I'm at his house to listen. I have to exercise detachment and tolerance. I must be shockproof. I must save my reactions for later because, if I appear to be affected, he'll find an excuse to stop.

And yes, there are risks for him too. Will he show his feelings and then regret it? Will he feel my presence as intrusive? Will he realise there's more he wants to say? More I want to hear?

The fact is there's some deception in my agreeing to listen to his life story. I'm not doing this just to help him. I have my own agenda. I want to read him as I listen. I want to find out what is between the lines. I'll be searching for clues.

I'm also here to put the boundaries back where they should be. Normally I feel like a child when I'm in his presence, but by working with him on this project, perhaps I can hold on to the person I have become, the person he doesn't know and now never will. He's too old and he's left it too late.

Soon, maybe in a matter of months, his life will end and I'll have to survive. Before he goes, I want to know who he is, who he says he is, even perhaps glimpse who he could have been. I need to examine my inheritance, by looking at his. I'm trying to find morsels of truth in the way he describes things, in the stories he tells, in the lies. He assumes he's in control, but this time, at last, he might be wrong because I know a lot more than he does about the business of writing.

I'm intoxicated by a sense of power and danger, courage and fear. Part of me thinks I shouldn't go anywhere near him and part of me has to go. I'm playing with fire and I know it. Philip says I shouldn't be doing this and, if I must, I have to be very, very careful. But there's a reckless part of me. I tell Philip not to worry.

* * *

27

THE WORLD ACCORDING TO MY FATHER
1. INHERITANCE
(see also *Anger, Gifts, Money*)

Most things are inherited and it is best to accept this.

A person can inherit good things: money, land and property,
furniture, pictures. A name.

Of course looks and personality are inherited too. There are
family features that are obvious – nose, height, teeth, intelligence.
These can be a sign of belonging.

The problem about inheritance is that you rarely get what you
want, and when you do there's usually someone else who wants
it too and is prepared to say so, and that person may want to
squabble over it. This detracts from the pleasure and satisfaction
of inheritance.

One way or another, disease and cause of death seem to be inherited
too, not that we talk about that. Still, you can't help noticing. If
you're born to be hung you'll never be drowned.

* * *

He chooses to begin at the beginning. *Because it is logical,* he
says. He will start with his childhood.

I put a new audio-tape into the machine and press the red
button. He's live.

His voice is gritty nowadays with rough lower tones, at times harsh. His Oxford accent seems more pronounced than I remember, perhaps because he's consciously wanting to sound like a radio announcer. He's assumed the role of storyteller and he's good at it.

He begins by reaching back well before his childhood, to his own father's early life. The third child of a minor baronet, the young Samuel Best worked as a jackaroo in New Zealand in the final decade of the nineteenth century before going to India to become a tea-planter. He married Evelyn May in 1914. My father relates how he was the youngest of their four children. His sister, Joy, was eight years his senior, then came Robert known as Bobby, and then John. My father was born on the fifth of October 1923, three years after John.

He never really had a relationship with his father, he says. His father was fifty when he was born, a remote figure who was often away, particularly after his first wife (my father's mother) died. And anyway, he took no interest at all in his youngest child.

One of my father's earliest memories is of playing make-believe on the balcony of a London hotel with his mother's walking stick over his shoulder as a rifle. Or has the memory come from a photograph? He's not sure. They were all staying in London because his mother needed medical treatment there.

The next memory is of playing in the garden with his cousin when his aunt comes to tell him his mother has died. He is five.

Then he remembers being left for some months with a woman who complains about her painful feet.

He recalls going to a boys' boarding school in Hampshire when he's six. There, he's beaten for not working at his Latin. He is the only boy whose parents never come to visit him, or take him out to lunch or tea.

A widow called Daisy makes *a dead set* at his father and they marry a year after his mother's death. Daisy wants his father's money, everyone says so. But his father doesn't really have much money. Still – what he has, she spends. She has an extension built on to the family home at Merrow, near Guildford, destroying his mother's drawing room and providing space for her own two children.

She is, in my father's words, *an abominable woman.* He cannot understand why his father married her. *Perhaps because she was very good in bed*, he suggests.

I am cold now, sitting here, watching his face in the low winter light, an old man's features overrun with rare emotional weather, the result of his recollections of a distant past.

I am listening as I have never listened to his stories, as though they are the last stories I'll ever hear. I half hope he'll stop, half fear he won't, but he goes on and on and on, for over an hour. No pauses, no need for prompts. The narrative comes out whole. He is fluent and articulate, as if he's been rehearsing it all his life. And as the words rise, the damage in him floats to the surface and rests there, so that during this time he is with me in a way he has never been before. He is present, engaged, interested in what he's saying, committed to communicating it. He is more alive with the pain at the surface like this. And there's no need for him to stop and listen, or interact, which he doesn't do naturally at the best of times.

Then suddenly, as he's approaching a time towards the end of his school career, he falters. He misses one of his own cues. There's the slightest crack in his voice. It's over. *Let's stop there, shall we? I need a drink.*

Later he tells me he's not sure if he'll want to continue. He says, *I will listen to today's tape and make an evaluation.*

* * *

```
Transcript:
So it was a rather isolated beginning. I don't
remember really anything happening until I was
in the bushes with Rowland Eustace at Stoodwell
in Merrow and I can remember Stella, his mother,
coming up and saying, Patrick I am sorry to
tell you that your mother has died. So that
must have been 1929 and I was five at the time.
```

* * *

My father's loss in 1929 was grievous. I have always wondered how he experienced his mother's death. He probably didn't go to her funeral. Did he realise that he would never see her again?

There are times in all our lives when we have just lost something forever, but we aren't properly aware of the loss. This hiatus may last minutes or hours, days or decades.

Then there may be times, later on, when we see that what we lost has reappeared, perhaps in a different form. Perversely, this may be the moment when we feel the original loss most acutely.

Between these two points, between the loss and the rediscovery, is the disturbance – the nightmare of the search that is seemingly endless. I think my father may have spent his life looking for his mother and his home.

We search for lost things and we search for patterns. We search by telling ourselves and one another stories. They are works of love and creativity but also of fury and grief.

* * *

31 October, 2008
I'm thinking of Halloween, 1995. The date my Freddie was due. He was born two days later but that final waiting seemed to last forever.

Dad tells me he wants to go to Switzerland. He's far too ill to travel. I try to suggest this but he won't accept it. He wants to see mountains again, and lakes. He needs to feel the alpine air sharp in his lungs.

I'll do what I bloody well like, he says.

* * *

As he says this I'm remembering the last time I was in the mountains. It was Christmas 2005. Philip and Freddie and I were briefly with my father and brothers in Klosters before the three of us went on over the Bernina pass to Santa Catarina, high in the Italian Alps. Beautiful and barren. It was the coldest skiing I've ever known, twenty-three degrees below freezing at three thousand metres, too cold to stay out more than an hour, too cold to take off your gloves without risking frostbite.

We stayed in the village to watch the local circus and the fireworks on New Year's Eve and then travelled north again on New Year's Day.

At Campocologno, just above Tirano, the train trundled up the village street like a tram, past frozen washing and empty window baskets and flaking paint, winding its way up and up, finally rolling over the Bernina pass. As it went higher, it turned through apple orchards and sang its way past vines, making a sound like a finger sliding round the wetted rim of a glass. From the window I saw trees growing strong and upright, but anchored in mountain rubble and pine needles. I saw the front of the train ahead of us as we twisted up to the snow line.

At Val Poschiavo, near the pass, there was Miralago again. When we'd come down this way a week previously, the lake had been all bright ice and smooth concealment so that you couldn't tell what was underneath. Now the lake ice had begun to melt and in the shadow of the mountains the water was black. There were rippling images of silver birch and snowy peaks where before there had been whiteness and trickery.

All my life I've loved snow. I was seduced by it in Swiss alpine villages and over distant snowfields and glaciers. I loved that landscape as the others in my family loved it, for its cold that numbs your fingers and its light that burns your eyes. I loved speeding over the snow's beguiling surfaces. I liked the glitter and changefulness, the fact that you had to pit your wits against the whiteness because you couldn't trust it to hold you or tell you where you were. Snow never did the same thing twice. It could not be relied on.

I learned all that as a child, but now I like to see through the snow to the rock and grass and mud underneath. Miralago in a thaw, rather than a freeze. The feeling, as opposed to the numbness.

* * *

Ciné film, 1961

The back half of a mammoth truck tilts so that its cargo of snow is dumped at the side of the road. Slowly, slowly, the grey heap shifts downwards. Then the lorry returns to the upright position. Shots of mountains and of monochrome chocolate ads and of jelly-mould cars in station car parks. Long, winding trains. Shots of anonymous skiers wearing tapered ski trousers and thigh-length anoraks with hoods, raising drinks over scrubbed wooden tables. Trays of food served by smiling Swiss women in white blouses, dirndl skirts and lace-up leather ankle boots. Footage of bleached-out mountain ridges, cols, glaciers and peaks, seen always from left to right and then from right to left – a meticulous searching panning action, almost level and admirably steady.

* * *

This is the place where my father seemed happiest to use his Bolex ciné camera. Switzerland: silent, and all the people there jerky and busy but silent too, speaking in strange unheard but familiar words, just beyond lip-reading. For my father, it was a place of ham sandwiches and beer and this skiing holiday with my mother.

Authentic period dust is trapped around the edges of this moving world. Flashes of violet and pale orange break like small explosions at the boundaries of my father's vision – accidents of light and processing, aberrations in the filmic weather.

Occasionally a crude line, a jolt in the action, tells of his hours of editing on Sunday evenings.

He wasn't to be disturbed. He was doctoring the films. He had the power to alter our world.

I've watched these films many times now and still I'm puzzled by the order. Transfers between different media over more than fifty years (ciné film to video tape, video tape to DVD) have probably reordered the narrative so the sequence isn't as it originally was. Occasionally we children grow older only to become younger again. Dogs regress to puppyhood. Winter reverts to autumn.

Even in my father's heyday, footage was occasionally lost. There were premieres at family Christmases when he set up all the equipment to show his latest work, calling my mother to come from the kitchen where the chestnuts or sprouts were keeping her. Sometimes the reel stuck on the projector and we children screeched as the light burned out an image, melting it in front of our eyes, in glorious colour. My mother cried out. My father cursed. Parts of the film were gone forever. The rest would have to be respliced later. Meanwhile, he would reload the film onto the projector wheel and carry on.

Lights on, lights off again. He used to get so frustrated. I could tell he was glad when it was all over and he could relax with a drink.

* * *

6 November, 2008
The operation postponed from last week is being done today. Dad is first on the surgeon's list.

I went over last Friday. I was there in good time to take him for his pre-op blood tests but although I arrived half an hour before the appointment, he'd already left to drive himself the five minutes to the doctors' surgery. I followed him, parked and found him in the waiting room.

He was angry. *You're terribly late.*

I rode it out this time, not willing to be pulled into the trap. I said, *I always keep my promises, Dad.*

Later, over lunch, I tried to talk with him about finding a carer, someone to help with things like getting him to medical appointments and doing some of the shopping and the errands.

I'm not ill. Stop making a fuss, he said, pouring more claret.

* * *

My father has always been early. The kind of early that means he'll comfortably catch the flight or train before the one he planned to catch, and the one he planned to catch would have left swathes of time before the meeting or funeral or appointment. Punctuality for my father is about being very early and not minding all the knock-on effects – the long cold wait on the platform, the locked door of the shop that's still closed, or the embarrassment of the host who isn't ready for you.

My mother tended towards the other end of the spectrum of readiness, but whether by nature or because she felt the need to pull against the tide of my father's earliness, I never knew. Not that she was unpunctual but she had a magical way of being ready in time, without a fuss, and presenting herself calmly and correctly within the polite range of punctual – a minute or two later than an appointed time but about an hour later than my father's sense of punctuality would dictate.

This difference was, of course, a source of tension between them. Every departure for a holiday, every family trip to London, every party or event triggered wave upon wave of stress around the timing. My father's expectations were never met, my mother felt harassed and pressured, and we children were caught in the middle. We learned to keep our heads down and our mouths shut until the journey or day was well under way. And because, according to my father's internal clock, we were perpetually somehow running late, there was never any margin for unscheduled halts or special requests. Woe betide you if you needed to relieve yourself outside the appointed stop-offs.

I wonder what was at the root of my father's sense of timing. Was he trying to prevent nasty surprises by keeping ahead of schedule? I've often pictured him, a small boy playing with his cousin in his aunt's garden, when she comes to tell him that his mother has died. He's completely unprepared for this and for the rest of his life. How could it be otherwise? He was born too late to share more than five years with his own mother. From now on he will always arrive well before he needs to.

* * *

Ciné film, 1961
Daymer Bay, Cornwall. The tide is out. Rock pools, beach cricket, coloured tents ranged across the sands. The girl wears a pink polka-dot bikini. The tall woman with long legs – the nanny – walks her over the beach towards the ripples. They step together into the water. The girl looks up at the woman, then jumps up and down ecstatically. But this footage for some reason is slower than the rest, so the child appears to move in slow motion, hovering above each ripple before landing again, her hands flapping fast-slow at her sides in excitement. The camera pans left to right, and right to left, along the horizon, to the peninsulas either side of the bay, lingering on

the headland and cliffs to the left. Cut to the Corcovado Mountain, Rio de Janeiro, zooming in on the figure of Christ the Redeemer.

* * *

15 November, 2008

Dad was pale today as he told me the results of the recent tests and biopsies. There's another tumour near the right kidney. He has twinges of pain in his groin and down his right leg.

Again he mentioned the cliff. *Do you remember it? That marvellous place, just you and me and the gulls?* What's he trying to tell me by repeatedly alluding to it? He recalls it and I'm persuaded by the strength of his recollection. For as long as I listen to his account, I live in his truth. But his truth isn't mine. I sometimes have trouble realising that.

I thought about it more, after I left his house. Clearly he liked going to the cliff hideaway then and he likes recalling it now. But for me the memory of being with him at the cliff is the edge of my fear.

I liked being sought out by him because I always wanted to please him. Pleasing him made something seem better. I do know that.

The Cornish cliff is colour and landscape and that's what holds my attention as I try to remember. The place itself steadies my gaze. The stirring sea, the blue sky, the clouds moving constantly as they did yesterday and will again tomorrow.

* * *

The more often he tells me his remembered version of the cliff hideaway, the more I want my own. I try to imagine it, try to take myself back there so I have a memory too.

We had probably returned to the holiday house from the morning surf, rinsed off the salt and sand, changed into jeans and T-shirts and woollen jumpers.

Then he would have said, *Shall we go to our favourite place?*

And I would have said, *Yes, Daddy.*

I suppose we went to the cliff on our way somewhere else, perhaps as part of an expedition to buy groceries from the village shop. So we might have set off from the house with a purse and a string bag and possibly a list written in my mother's softly rounded hand: Brillo pads, cornflakes, baked beans, sausages. We would have left the garden through the blue gate in the corner and traversed the gently shelving turf, turning right onto the cliff path.

To find the approach to our secret place, we must have negotiated a fence. This wouldn't have been difficult since the wire was low and even my short legs could manage the step over it. But then there was a narrow track through bracken and gorse as tall as me. Here my father would have given me the string bag to hold and then he'd have swung me up to sit astride his shoulders.

The sea spread out before us like a great sheet of beaten pewter, and there was the cliff edge, or at least the first edge, the one we would have to drop below to get to our hidden ledge.

Suddenly the remembering stops. I can only recall the landscape, not the two of us in it.

* * *

I remember the day my father brought home a barrel of butter from Denmark. I was seven. A cool afternoon in Sussex, our first spring at Manor Farm, and my mother led all four children out onto the lawn.

We sat in a circle, the five of us. She wore a pink-and-grey dress and she spooned butter into our mouths. We shared the wooden spoon and the pale creamy butter, unsalted. She spooned until the barrel was empty and we were full.

That's all. Each time I play the footage in my head it's the same, but – no, not the same. Each time a little more stretched, distorted, the green perhaps a shade or two faded from the green the grass was last time. Might the memory eventually snap, like my father's ciné films on the projector? Is this why I want to preserve it and not think of it too often?

And yet I do want to. This memory brings news of the child I was, the child who is still somewhere inside me. It's her memory.

I see the grass is green. I hear my mother's laugh. I sense my three brothers. I can't picture them but I know their mouths open and close around the wooden spoon, as mine does. It's a tight circle.

I see the black metallic hoops around the outside of the barrel. I taste the sweet clammy butter, rough on my tongue.

The scene ends, each time, when the little barrel is emptied. I peer in as my mother tips it towards me to show me. There's only the dark oily wood.

I need to recall this scene simply to know that it happened, to know that on a certain day in perhaps April 1963, we sat together in a circle and my mother fed us butter, concentrated milk, a precious melting Danish gold.

I can still see the spoon dip into the barrel, come up with

another scoop of warm, soft primrose light, greasy now in the sun as it comes towards my mouth. My mother smiling over us.

I am homesick for this: the beginning, the butter, the spoon, the cool air. The faithful, solemn taking of turns until all the butter is gone.

* * *

THE WORLD ACCORDING TO MY FATHER
2. APPETITE

Something to be suspicious of, to control, to tease out.

No snacks between meals.

Meals may be postponed almost indefinitely if there is plenty to drink (see *Alcohol*). It is better to eat a meal tepid with the right appetite than hot when you're not yet hungry.

Appetite should be denied and indulged, alternately.

A person's own appetites are the ones that matter most, but this must not appear so, hence manners should be assiduously cultivated.

Appetites for alcohol, savoury dishes and bitter chocolate are acceptable. Appetites for milk shakes, puddings, cake and dried fruit are suspect.

* * *

I watched more of the ciné films yesterday afternoon and last night, starting with the films when I was about three or four and going right through to the end when I was fourteen or fifteen. I felt again what I often feel: the abrupt change at age seven or eight when my hair is cut short. This occurs by chance between the first DVD and the second. It's just a coincidence, of course, the way the films are split neatly across the two disks.

I watched the child I was on the first disk and cried. I cried for the lively little girl who always wants to hop and jump about without her clothes, constantly on the move, gesturing and communicating non-stop with herself and everyone around her. An extrovert, playing up to the camera. I've lost her. I've lost who she might have been. There's a parallel life somewhere, a life she had that I didn't. I've been cheated.

Later, on the second disk, there's the quieter, introverted child. The camera is on her less. She doesn't deserve it, doesn't want it. When she is framed, she sits apart from the others with her head in a book, turns away from the camera or covers her face with her hand.

Which film is true? Which child is me?

* * *

You're sitting at the kitchen table. Sunday lunch, 1964. Your mother has cooked roast chicken with fat rashers of bacon draped over the breasts to keep them moist and roast potatoes and her famous gravy made with Bisto and Marmite. There are boiled carrots and Brussels sprouts in hot Pyrex dishes. Your father has sharpened the carving knife and sets about dividing the bird. He'll sit at the head of the table. You'll sit on his right, as usual, your elder brothers on his left. Your mother will be at the other end with your younger brother next to her.

You've already seen what will follow. Your favourite pudding. Lemon mousse in those little glass dishes on stems. Eight of them lined up on a tray in the pantry. You spotted them when you fetched the carrots.

On top of each swirl of pale yellow is a glacé cherry, gently pressed into the mousse, just enough so it will stay put with the mousse setting around it. The cherries are bright red with a gloss of syrup. You love their colour and the way they aren't like real cherries at all. The first thing you'll do when the dish is put in front of you is push your cherry to the bottom and pretend you don't know it's there. Later, you'll relish the surprise of finding it when you get to the last few spoonfuls, something shiny and delicious. Buried treasure. The best, left until last.

This is what you do each time. A ritual. And each time, he plays his game. He waits until you've eaten almost all the mousse, until the prize is visible in the bottom of your dish, and then he nudges you, points with his left hand to something high up in the corner of the room. An imaginary butterfly or a bee. And as you look up, his right hand comes quickly with his spoon and scoops out the cherry from your dish and delivers it to his own mouth, even though he doesn't like sweet things. You hear his laughter. By the time you look down, it's all over. Until next time.

I wonder now at the endless repetition. The normality of it. I wonder at the contract that must have existed between us: my hiding the cherry, his stealing it. My trust, his power. The need

43

for me to be gullible. His need to take from me. My obligation to accept what he did.

* * *

Ciné film, 1963

Spring at Manor Farm. Panning shot of a dense patch of azaleas in bloom – pinks, oranges, yellows, all bowing and swaying in the spring breeze. Zoom to a mature magnolia and a bright pink prunus by the high-banked lawn that used to be a tennis court. Now it's summer. The 1930s concrete pool at the bottom of the garden is full of water with children splashing in it. They swim the breaststroke and use car inner tubes for rubber rings, diving in and out of them. There's a Lilo boat too, blue and orange. They take it in turns to sit in the boat while the others pull them around. The children's heads are clearly in focus but since the undoctored spring water is green and cloudy, their naked bodies are visible below the surface only as shadows. Blurred and strangely tapered, they might belong to fish or mermaids. Cut to a tilt shot where a grinning boy in black trunks opens his cupped hands to display a crested newt. He sets it down on the flagstones. It scuttles out of shot.

* * *

Each autumn we drained the pool. The whole family spent a weekend scrubbing the rough concrete walls and floor with stiff bristle brushes to remove the algae. By then, most of the newts had gone down the drain with the water, but there were usually a few left behind. We raced them on the slippery base of the pool, holding back the largest newts by their tails and letting go of the smaller ones first.

All the films of this period are of the garden and the outside of the house. Cousins, friends, pets, all appear and disappear on the terrace and lawns. Children grow and change, hemlines go up. These things happen against the backdrop of the house, its windows closed and black in contrast to the scenes of spring and summer colour.

When I went back to Manor Farm in 2005, the first time in thirty-two years, it felt like going backstage. Here was the oak-panelled dining hall we never used for meals but where my mother installed a half-size billiard table for my brothers. Here was the dark hallway where we took our formal meals on Sundays, and at Christmas and Easter. The drawing room with its grandiose bay window onto sloping lawns. My father's study where he spent his Sunday evenings editing the ciné films.

Placing my hand on the banister to climb the stairs, I knew a moment of pre-panic, a physical surge like the feeling when you're overtaking and think you might not make it back to your own side of the road in time to avoid an oncoming car.

Returning to this house was painful and difficult. It always had been. Of course there was the initial excitement of coming home from school but as soon as we arrived, and then throughout the holidays, a trunk was parked outside each of our bedrooms. We had to take out items of school uniform that needed cleaning or mending or naming. My mother put them back in the trunk when the job was done. Towards the end of the holidays, books, shoes, wellington boots, tuck and new items of clothing would be packed. At this stage the trunk lids were left open, so my mother could drop things in as she passed. How I hated this permanent state of impermanence, this way of being between school terms.

* * *

28 November, 2008

I'm waiting for Dad. He's coming to my house today for the second session of talking about his life. I don't really know how I feel about this next meeting, I don't even know what I want from it. I'm numb.

He has begun in his own way. It's neither the story of how he feels nor the story of who he is. It certainly isn't the story of what's beautiful or what fascinates him. It's a crossword puzzle with a single column of clues and because he's supplied only one dimension, somehow I must work out the other.

I'd like to think of my life as part of an ongoing story so a narrative might help me, but my mother has died having forgotten where she came from and my father, so far, has given only a brief account of his early life. I want more of his story, partly to help me understand him but mostly to help me piece together my own life.

The floor is swept. I have dressed carefully for him. I will listen to him. We will continue to behave almost normally with each other, despite everything.

He arrives with the notes he's made and then he talks straight onto tape. From time to time I ask a question, but mostly he speaks fluently, without any prompting. He really is a natural.

* * *

```
My brothers, Bobby and John, used to build
houses underground. I say houses but they were
like trenches. And all I remember is they were
beautifully built of wood and the two of them
used to spend a lot of time doing this and
being down there, because like me they didn't
like being in the house very much with Daddy's
second wife Mater as she was called. She was
difficult. We would rather keep out of her way
as much as possible. But I remember asking John
once when he was down in his underground house,
Can I come down? and he said, No, no, no this
is for Bobby and me — you are much too young.
So I was excluded.
```

* * *

I'm the only one there when he tells his story. It's perhaps my truest role in that family. I'm the one who takes what is said and written, as well as what's not said and not written, and I try to make something of it. I listen for truth, collecting the words, looking after them.

There are the characters in a story and there's the writer. Part of me was lost and another part became the searcher and onlooker, listener and interpreter. I'm the seer, and I'm the hearer of voices.

* * *

Some things don't change. Like KitKat and Coca-Cola and the song of blackbirds, or the way you feel when the heat of the new spring sun warms your back. But it's an illusion, a trick. The lettering on the wrapper and the red of the can have been subtly altered and so have the recipes. The blackbirds and the skin have died and been replaced.

There were periods in my childhood when nothing seemed to change. I remember the frustration of it. Another term at school, just like the last, another seaside holiday, more pink calamine lotion on my sunburnt neck and the tops of my feet, the same jokes around the table. Tomato mince and mash for Saturday lunch. Childhood was a wheel, a trap, and there seemed to be no way out.

It was a long time before I understood enough about dysfunctional families to realise that the stasis – the not allowing things to change, one way or another – enabled us to keep working through the underlying choreography of our disease.

My mother had married an orphan, as she liked to put it. She looked after my father as though he was one of her children. And emotionally he was more of a sibling to us than a parent. My father had married someone who must and would be his first reliable woman, someone to depend on, who would never desert or betray him, a blend of mother, sister, nanny and girl-next-door. She wanted a lot of babies. He probably wanted to be her only child but he also wanted to please her, so she won.

Normally the first-born is emotionally privileged, at least for a while. But Christopher, having arrived promptly with the Christmas goose in 1948, was soon supplanted by Michael who lived little more than a year before dying from an intestinal infection and dehydration, in a few agonising days in June 1952.

As a child, Christopher had his own serious health problems. He was often neglected and misunderstood. And he was sent to boarding school at the age of six. It was a grim re-enactment of my father's own desolate childhood.

All the while my mother was grieving for Michael, the perfect baby, the special one, the one she surely hadn't looked after properly. In his leaving, he had proved that parents have to keep a tight grip on the lives of their children.

David was born in 1953, a plump, carefree cherub, all smiles and cuddles. My mother often told me, *It was a miracle. That was when I came back to life.*

I arrived in 1955, the only girl, my father's sugarplum fairy, heiress to my mother's feisty female line.

The youngest, Philip, was born in 1960, just as Christopher edged towards puberty and was being fitted with uniform for his seventh boarding school.

* * *

THE WORLD ACCORDING TO MY FATHER
3. ALCOHOL

An antidote to pain of all kinds.

An aid to forgetting.

A way of oiling the social wheels.

Something to look forward to.

A habit not to be relinquished.

There is no problem that alcohol does not ease, no experience that it does not enhance.

It is undignified for a woman to have too much to drink.

* * *

10 December, 2008

Dad's in hospital. His pain suddenly became severe and he was a danger to himself at home, self-medicating with large quantities of oral morphine and alcohol. The doctors can't get to the bottom of it. According to them, he shouldn't be in pain because there's no medical reason for it. They're trying to stabilise him so he can go home in time for Christmas.

It's tricky. With my brothers so far away and Dad's friends phoning me to report on his state of health, I feel the full weight of responsibility. I can't pretend he's not my father. I'm the one who is expected to look after him, the dutiful only daughter who lives close enough to visit regularly. Besides, it's what I've always done, despite everything. As though I believe that if I keep doing 'the right thing' then that will make things better. It's a trap and I'm caught in it.

Yesterday when I went to see him he was rambling, confabulating, sometimes incomprehensible. One minute he was shouting at the nurses, asking the doctors to shoot him, put him out of his agony, *Which one of you has got the gun?* The next he was a small boy. I waited for a lull, a chance to raise again the subject of carers and persuade him that he can't be at home on his own. He got angry and shouted at me.

Later I remembered how he was packed off to boarding school when his father remarried. An unwanted woman was imported into his mother's home, his home. *That abominable woman.* He's not going to go through that again. No way will he agree to an unwanted strange woman being brought into his home.

* * *

```
Transcript:
Mater really upset everybody. Me in particular
because as the youngest, I was really the only
one who was at home. There was a lovely drawing
room in the house which was Mummy's favourite
room — her furniture, her curtains and all
these things that she really stamped with her
personality. And Mater turned it into a sort
of boys' room and built on a new drawing room
to the house.
```

* * *

12 December, 2008
I spend a little time every day singing, it helps me clear my head.

I sing within the walls I'm so glad to return to, shutting the world out, leaving the world out. I sing the same songs over and over. Italian baroque love songs, light and playful. Something of their mood sinks into me. Sometimes I dance as I sing.

Today I even imagine a world without him in it.

Each note rises inside me before I release it onto the December air.

* * *

There are days when I am aware of the spirited child within me, the one my father always said was so difficult, even as a baby. He wrote only once in the scrapbook my mother kept. It was to mark my first birthday: *Heaven help he who marries this tornado. He will lead a rough life and I for one would not argue with her! A devilment that is fearful.*

And now, as so often in this process of his dying, I'm asking myself why I need to hammer out this part of the story, my part. Isn't it all past, long past, and gone?

Secrets are secret, isn't that right? But untold, they swell and infiltrate everything. I feel completely filled up with secrets. I know the secrets must be let out. I know I'm the only one who can do this but each time I think about telling, I stall and stall, while fear and anxiety spread like blood in water.

Sometimes I hear inside me the ghostly voice of the child he stole, the child I may never find, and I have to listen. I want her to talk until she has nothing left to say. I want to wake up one day and find the voice exhausted and then I'll know the grandest, longest silence. And I'll choose what to put into that silence.

I'm clearer now about what makes me anxious. I'm starting to name some of these things: kisses, dentists, small spaces, dusk in an empty house, doors opening over carpets in the night, appointments to meet someone, being watched when I want to be alone. Being anywhere close to my father. Numbness. Losing things, not being able to find lost things.

And I want to pull together the small child and the one who grew from what happened to her. They're separate, I know that, and I want them to become one. I want this more than anything.

I have to be able to remember before I can begin to forget.

* * *

It's early spring, with daffodils out in the garden. Manor Farm, where you live from age seven to eighteen. Mostly you remember mornings but today it's teatime. You're hungry and tired. Mummy's in London, taking Philip to see a doctor. Christopher and David are at boarding school. Nanny's not here, because it's her day off. Daddy's at home to look after you.

You go to the big room where you've set up your model garden on the green baize of the billiard table. He follows you, and for a while he watches you play. Then he takes your hand and says to go with him. Puts his finger to his lips. Something secret.

Now you're in the lavatory at the end of the downstairs passage. The door's closed, the room's warm and a bit damp, and the ceiling's far above your head. He's in there with you. He's locking the door, the key's turning, the same type of long key that's in all the doors in this house, not shiny, but dull brown metal. You hear the sure click in the lock.

It's cramped in here with two people. He smells of soil and he smells of smoke. You're cold in his shadow. His hands are heavy on your shoulders. Suddenly, one minute to the next, it's not daytime but night. Dark and quiet and tight.

The window's high up in the wall facing you. The door's behind you, that long key sticking into the top of your back. Neither door nor window is a way out. He's close. Looking up, you can't see the top of his face or his eyes, only his chin and nose. His hands are undoing his belt buckle, flicking back the leather. A rattle as the belt comes loose. He unzips his trousers and they fall down his white legs and lie in a heap on the lino. You're looking at his underpants now. White. You're wearing white pants too.

Close your eyes and open your mouth.

You do what he says.

You always do what he says. One of the first things he taught you was the meaning of obedience. *You must be obedient. Good girls do what they're told.*

There's a thing in your mouth. It's alive and fleshy. He's forcing it in further and further. He takes it out then shoves it back in. One of his hands is at the back of your neck, stroking your hair, pulling your head forwards. Your jaws have to open wider, wider. Their hinges will break. You can't breathe. It tastes horrible. You're going to be sick. The key cuts into your shoulders. It hurts, it hurts.

Keep your eyes shut.

Later, you turn away to cry.

He says, *Don't cry, let me wipe your tears.*

* * *

I deduced long ago that I was between seven and eight years old when this happened. Other memories – the sort that are physical feelings and nightmares rather than pictures or sounds – tell me that this wasn't the beginning. And it certainly wasn't the end.

I can't reach some memories, or can only partially reach them, and that's both better and worse. Better because I don't know exactly what happened, worse also because I don't know exactly what happened. Worse still because I know something toxic remains locked away.

I held this particular memory for many years before I was sure it was him. The certainty came slowly and painfully. There are other similar memories from around this time, with strong visual elements, even full sensory recall. If I'm feeling robust, I can come and go from them and interrogate them. I feel a sense of control because I can choose when to close them down.

The process of remembering has been long and halting. It began after what we'd nowadays call a triggering event. I was called to jury service at the Old Bailey in the early 1990s and served in a child sex abuse case. That traumatic experience prompted a new kind of remembering. At first, thoughts and sensations started to surface. I tried to ignore them but they became more insistent, so I had to engage with them. I experienced accompanying bouts of anxiety, depression and insomnia. Then the flashbacks and nightmares came, and a raft of mystery symptoms and illnesses like those in my childhood. It was some years before I could make any sense of what was happening and before I could acknowledge these memories for what they were.

More recently, my remembering has been facilitated by psychotherapy and by writing. The pressure and urgency of witnessing my father's decline has caused an acceleration which can be alarming but it is also helpful. It brings more clarity.

* * *

THE WORLD ACCORDING TO MY FATHER
4. DENIAL

There is simply no such thing.

This does not exist.

This never happened.

* * *

I learned to put things in containers and the containers in other containers. To hold things safe and private.

My mother had a jewellery box, pale brown suede with a brass lock and key, and a small carrying handle. I have it still. In the top right corner of the lid the initials S.P.F. are stamped in gold gothic letters, so worn now that only the deepest parts of the imprints still hold flakes of gold.

The box first belonged to Sophie Fairley, or Little Granny as my mother called her. Little Granny waited seven years for my great-grandfather to come back from India and marry her, then they were together just a few years before he died. My grandfather Hamilton was their only child. He married my mother's mother, Phyllis, in London in 1913, and sailed his bride off to India. My mother, Heather Elizabeth, their second child, was born in 1924, three years after her sister, Auriol.

The jewellery box was a story book. It held not only fragments of Sophie Fairley's story but elements of my grandmother's too. Small trinkets, miniature carved ivory elephants, lockets with photographs, odd earrings and gold chains were all chapters of their stories passed on to me by my mother. And then, of course, there were my mother's own stories, and these she would also tell me when we sat together on her bed and looked through the contents of the box.

I suppose I was four or five the first time my mother showed me the jewellery box. I came into her bedroom one afternoon when she was sitting at her dressing table, the leather case open in front of her. I must have stood at her elbow and begun to ask her: *What's this Mummy? Where did this come from? Why are there two of these?* And she would have answered with mysterious words, foreign names of faraway places, tales of love and long sea journeys, teasing out for me the complicated ties of family and other relationships, until finally she would give me a reason to stop – bathtime or teatime, or time for her to get dressed up and go out with my father.

Then she'd close the box, open the top right drawer of her dressing table and place it carefully inside. As she pushed the drawer in, she'd kiss me on the forehead and I felt the double emotions of joy and loss. There was another feeling too – a sense that this was something to be looked forward to. To be repeated. I loved the expectation, the repetitions. While I waited for our next session, my excitement grew until I could barely contain it.

Sometimes when I asked, she refused, saying, *It's too late in the evening,* or, *We only looked yesterday,* or, *Your father's waiting for me downstairs, I mustn't be late.* Or occasionally, *I don't feel like it just now.*

Once, on a warm summer evening just before my eighth birthday, I asked her after my bath when she was combing my hair. She told me, *No, not now, it makes me too sad.* I had no idea what to make of this. Looking in the box with my mother was the essence of delight. I had her to myself, we shared something that she didn't, to my knowledge, share with anyone else. Every telling of every story brought me closer to her and made me feel safe with her, which was what I craved. If this made me happy, how could it make her sad? I thought the sadness must be my fault so I didn't ask again for several months. I felt shut out, guilty.

Perhaps it was while I couldn't look in her jewellery box that I began to make my own imaginary box where I could keep secrets and stories. Lying in bed at night I'd go over the objects, like a litany, as I inspected each one in my memory:

The screw-top ivory pill-box with thread so fine you can hardly believe it was carved by hand. Inside are diamond earrings Mummy wears to London; the brooch called gold doggy that Ced gave Granny in Assam; silver Canadian Air Force wings; a gold locket with a picture of a man wearing a bow-tie; a brooch made of miniature knitting needles with dark-blue wool and a miniature sock attached, given to Mummy by Joe; the soft leather pouch with Indian coins inside; a little card with Mummy's name written on, from her twenty-first birthday party at the Dominion Officers' Club; a pearl ring with diamonds given to Mummy by John's mother, a famous actress in the War – poor John was killed or he might have been my Daddy; an earring made of jet, all black in the shape of a tear, Granny got it in Paris when she was a young woman.

Later that year, when I was once again looking inside the leather box, I dared at last to ask my mother how it could make her sad. She said, *Looking at these things reminds me of all the lives I might have lived, all the lives your Granny and my Little Granny might have lived.* Her answer satisfied me. As far as I could tell, those thoughts, those alternative lives, were quite safe in there and that was all that mattered.

* * *

Transcript:
The school was right on top of the hill at Ringwood. It was perishingly cold. I used to get the most terrible blisters on my hands. And playing games was agony. What I do remember is, when I finally got to bed in the evening, getting in between the sheets and bicycling like hell to get some heat. It was a very cold house. The Headmaster was a man called Andrews. He had a daughter who was one of the Mistresses and I remember she was well developed, I suppose because I was beginning to get interested in that sort of thing. I had a crush on her.

And the Headmaster Andrews was very keen on moths. So right at the top of the house he built a special room with very strong lights and every morning he went up there to see what moths had come in during the night and he bottled them up, you know with whatever you kill moths with in the jar, and showed them to us. And they were wonderful. Some of them had about six-inch wingspans you know, very beautiful.

* * *

Is it like this?

My brothers' domain. *In,* where I shouldn't go. Spitfires and Messerschmitts hang on threads in the darkening air.

Isn't it like this? The quiet afternoon. Trestle table drawing-pinned with paper, littered with Airfix paints. Camouflage Grey, Khaki Drab. Pots of sable-hair brushes. Tubes of glue. A half-built Russian tank. Dead bluebottles. Daddy longlegs everywhere.

Hard to strike a match against the little strip. I try and try. At last it flashes into life, sears my thumb. Drop it. Smoulder smoke, then flaring print, flames scorching the Russian tank. A bottle of water – quick quick – unscrew the cap – pour – but *Oh! Oh! Oh!* – the liquid fuels the fire, makes it gasp and leap to the boarded ceiling in a rush of light and heat.

Beyond fear now. Part of me stays to watch the fire take – red, orange, yellow in a fiery fountain – whoosh – frizzle – spit. Part of me runs – down, along the passage, down more stairs to the kitchen, yelling, *Fire! Fire!* Out of breath.

And isn't it like this?

She turns from the sink, and she's past me, shouting, *Don't move!* Up, up, an angel to the top of the house. I didn't know she could fly.

Later she tells me she put the fire out with the big red extinguisher and her prayers. *And Never,* she says, *Never Never Never Never Again.*

Now I light matches in my head. Let them drop. I choose when to tip white spirit on the blaze. I stand at the centre, fire circling, wrapping, keeping me safe.

It is like this.

* * *

I was sent to my bedroom without supper after I started the fire in the attic at Manor Farm. I remember being hungry. I remember being terrified my mother might not love me anymore.

* * *

Ciné film, 1963
Again the garden at Manor Farm. Another view, this time from the bottom of the long sloping lawn, looking up. Red and yellow tulips in rows, moving in the wind. Behind the tulips a summer house with a shingled roof. Now the camera's eye settles on an upper lawn, at the top of a steep grass bank, and a huge tree, probably an oak. A swing on long ropes is attached to the tree. The girl swings, pushing her feet out as she moves forward over the bank, tucking them in as she goes back.

* * *

3 January, 2009
Dad's due any minute to record more of his story. I did suggest he might not be up to driving, but he insisted. Suddenly he's visiting my house more often. Is it this project that's changing something? He seems willing to travel to me.

I've lit a fire for him. I've hoovered and dusted as far into the house as I think he'll go. I've cleaned the loo and basin.

He's late today. He's never late. Since I woke up, I've had a keen fear of him having an accident on the way. Almost a premonition.

I think I'm afraid he'll die before I've heard him apologise.

It's raining hard. Surely he'll ring the buzzer soon. Then I'll go to the back gate and open it and tell him to be careful on the slippery red brick steps.

This morning I want to write his visit before he comes.

* * *

THE WORLD ACCORDING TO MY FATHER
5. GIFTS
(See *Money*)

It's better to give money and let the person choose something for him or herself.

Receiving a gift is embarrassing and may put a person in another person's debt.

If you have unwanted gifts, trade gifts or semi-used items you don't like or no longer need, these can be given as gifts to others.

* * *

4 January, 2009
I left the back gate open. Dad let himself in and from the dining room, where I was waiting, I heard his heavy knocking on the kitchen door.

My premonition was justified. He'd had a near miss in the heavy rain, narrowly escaping a collision on a roundabout. To avoid the crash, he was forced to take the wrong exit and it took him a while to backtrack.

He arrived white and shaken, but armed with the gift of a broken Sky set-top box to go with the satellite dish we don't have. He'd bought himself a new one and wanted me to have his old one.

I made him a cup of coffee. The first thing he told me was how he had worried after our last session. He said there were certain things he shouldn't talk about. Emotional things. Children, deaths. More than that. He had a particular look in his eyes – it's always there when he's about to tell you something he knows you don't want to hear. *But this is not my fault*, he expresses in that gaze. Or rather, *It is my fault but I'll not admit it.*

This whole visit was about avoidance. There was somewhere he was determinedly not going with his narrative. In the earlier session, focusing on his childhood and youth, he showed more of his feelings but only a small corner of the veil was lifted this time.

Before we started, he told me several times, *I'm not going to be talking about you children. Because that's another story.* He went on to give an account of his wartime years, his early career in the paper industry, his marriage to my mother, the arrival of children. When he announced he'd finished the session, I turned off the tape recorder.

He said, *There are other things too, but a man has a public life and a private life.*

I wanted to add, *And in your case, a secret life.*

* * *

We moved to Putney in 1939, I was sixteen. I was an Air Raid Warden at night, because people were in those days. And I used to go up to the City every morning and work in my father's offices in Fenchurch Street. They were difficult journeys because of all the bomb damage the previous night and there was masses of stuff burning and all that. So it was actually quite difficult to get to work. What I cannot remember is what happened with Daddy because he never came with me, so where was he? Did he sleep in the office, did he sleep in the City somewhere, did he stay in Putney? I don't think so. I remember him being in the office but it is a total blank what happened to him at night. Much of this time I didn't have friends and I spent too much time at home with Mater, just the two of us, and I don't remember Daddy being there. That's what puzzles me. So I was unhappy and I got more and more unhappy and when John, brother John, died in 1940 in his submarine off Norway, I decided that I would join the Navy. And I decided to fudge my age which was then 17 and I volunteered to join the Navy in the summer of 1941.

* * *

I was observing us, as I might observe a couple of strangers in the room. Between us was something too intimate and at the same time too distant. Put very simply: I knew him better than I should and he knew me better than he should, and there was no health in us.

I realised suddenly that I despised him. It was a terrible feeling, but it was right.

Part of me knew full well what he had done to me, and another part kept pushing and packing that knowledge away so that I could live the pretence of having a father I might be able to relate to. The truth of how he had treated me was something I could only glance at in flashes because that knowledge was too dangerous and too damaging. I could not cope with a permanent awareness of it.

I sat with him and he talked. As long as the past was falling apart in his voice and in his hands as he spoke, I was able to see through him, listen through him. He was becoming dust. With each layer of his emphasis and retelling, his stories were collapsing into one another, and my own truth was rising. I knew that.

* * *

A few years ago, changing trains at Clapham Junction, I was distracted for long enough to fall prey to a pickpocket who pressed against me in the crowd and took my wallet from my bag as I waited for the train doors to open.

The only thing I mourned (and still mourn) was a small black-and-white photograph, no more than three inches square, of me and my brother David as young children. I had been given the picture when I was twelve and had always kept it in my wallet.

It wasn't the kind of bright crisp image you'd see today of two small children waiting at the top of a slide or embracing on a summer beach, or posing with their heads together like conjoined twins. My snap was different.

My brother David, aged about six, is sitting up in bed, leaning back on pillows, looking straight at the camera. His small ghost face has currants for eyes and his hair falls over his forehead in a heavy shock but is cut short above the ears, in the fashion of the late 1950s. He wears long-sleeved, striped pyjamas, with plenty of room for growth. In front of him on the bed, there's a bed-tray on folding legs with the remains of a meal, perhaps breakfast: a cereal bowl, a cup. He seems disinterested in the meal.

The bed is a single bed with a wooden headboard and plain sheets. Behind the bed, bare walls. On my brother's right, there's a small dark-wood Windsor chair, where I'm sitting. If this is 1959, then I'm four years old. I too have a white face and currant eyes; I too look directly at the camera. My hair is brushed away from my temples and forehead, and gathered in a ponytail, though strands of shorter hair create a blur around my face. I'm wearing a collared shirt and shorts and white ankle socks. My hands rest in my lap.

Now, without the actual photograph, perhaps I can reinvent the image, even embellish what I recall. But to even think about doing that, I have to ask some questions. Is the bedroom door open or closed? Where does the daylight fall, or was the picture taken after dark? And where are the toys? I can't answer these questions and so I reject them. I want only the bare bones of the picture I knew so well. I want it like I want a glass of water when I'm thirsty. I want it back. The loss I feel over that minute piece of photographic evidence raises in me emotions so close and strong and fundamental that I'm again driven back to questions. Why do I want it? Why did I keep *this* picture and not another? What is its meaning for me?

What strikes me now is the way we inhabit the room, my brother in the bed, me on the chair, each of us in our place. We don't seem to relate to one another. There are no pictures on the walls, no window, no books on a shelf. We're simply here, in this bare room, sometime in 1959. And we're both focused intently on whoever is taking the photograph.

There's a strange but wonderful balance in the image: our matching dark eyes and white faces, our togetherness in isolation, the space between us, the mutual independence and the tacit agreement on distance. Everything held back and nothing said.

* * *

18 January, 2009
Can't stop thinking about Dad. A heady mix of my own frustration and anger at him is cocktailed with a weird and illogical compassion (his sadness released in me?). One minute I want him to die, I want him to go away, and especially I want him never to have been. Then I feel compelled to try and understand who he is, why he's like he is.

All this thinking seems to remake the world, shift the weather and the season, let rain fall and sun come through. A chaotic alchemy of telling and listening is at work. I've no idea yet what the outcome might be, though in odd moments I can see, in tiny shining glimpses, beyond all this history and beyond the present. To another life after my father's life has ended.

And where did my father's story and mine first truly intersect?

It wasn't when I was born. The flowers were in the fridge and my father was not there. It was a bit later, perhaps, when he first began to focus on me with that Bolex ciné camera.

* * *

Ciné film, 1956

The girl sits on the ground in a garden, next to a high chair. Red geraniums. Aluminium watering can.

A woman's arm places something on the seat of the high chair. A hand is held out to help the girl stand. She sees the treat, grabs it, sits back down to eat it. After three repetitions the woman places another treat on the chair seat and walks back a few paces away from the child, who pulls herself up by holding onto the rails of the high chair, scoops up the treat, sits down again with a thump.

* * *

6 February, 2009

Dad was here yesterday, the tenth anniversary of Mummy's death. We never mentioned her.

He's beginning to accept he's dying. He's reminiscing quite a bit. Perhaps this was his final visit. He brought me a plastic bag full of poppy seeds from his garden. For forgetting or remembering. For sleep and dreams. For pain relief or for death.

He was due to record one last episode of his life story but in the end he decided not to.

The recording sessions have been our relationship, the tape

recorder a third party, a facilitator, and now this silence feels final. No need for my friend, the machine. It is redundant. So is the blank tape. I have a strange urge to record something all on my own. To write on his blank sheet of paper.

Dad said he felt he had let me down by not recording the last session. I said it's not about what I want to do but about what he wants to do. The responsibility is his. I'm not letting him off that hook.

I feel stupid and disappointed, furious that I could fall into the trap of trusting him only to be betrayed again.

But anyway, the story is mine. I'll tell it my own way and he can't stop me.

* * *

Ciné film, 1957
She is walking steadily and purposefully now. She wears only socks and shoes and a pink sun hat, pushing a wheeled cart away across a yellow lawn. The camera follows her, zooms in, pulls back, zooms in again. Dimpled buttocks. Now she is leaning on a chair, still nude but for the socks and shoes and hat. She wiggles her bottom, side to side, side to side. The camera zooms in until her buttocks almost fill the frame. A forty-second close-up.

* * *

I am the storyteller and the story. I imagine myself into being. I invent my world every morning and take it apart each night when my mind switches off and the words settle silently at the base of the snow globe.

69

I was always fascinated by words. *Bath. Cup. Bed. Doll.* Words were magic: I said a word and that thing appeared. Sometimes saying the words made things come back when they had gone away. *Light. Mummy.* At night, when I had only the words, there was comfort in mouthing and miming them.

There were other kinds of words too of course. *Don't. Bad. Naughty.* These words brought feelings to the surface and made me frown or cry. My mother recorded in my scrapbook that I vehemently protested my virtue at an early age: *Me not naughty, you got to love me,* I would say.

I had a lot of feelings and they came bursting out with my words. If I was sitting in my high chair and banged my fist down hard and shouted *MORE*, I could feel how much I wanted something. But the grownups would *Ssshhhh* me or look the other way. Gradually, I learned not to give voice to some of my feelings but to keep them to myself.

A few key words seemed to have several effects at once, or made things happen quickly. The word *Sick* for instance. That word always made someone come running and I was caught up, lifted to a basin or lavatory bowl and held over it, swimming through air. I brought up the contents of my stomach in a heave and flood of sourness into the clean space. My ears popped and buzzed. My mouth burned. I was rinsed with water, my clothes were sometimes changed, and finally I was put back in the high chair. *Sick* often came after *Milk*, which was a word I didn't like at all.

When I was perhaps four or five, I began to understand the power of words and how they made extraordinary things happen. Saying words was like painting in those magic books with printed outlines of pictures. You dipped the brush in water and the colours appeared by themselves when you wetted the shapes on the paper. I could colour life by speaking what was welling up. I told my mother, *I love you*, and she would take me in her arms and hold me so close I could breathe in the soap and perfume on her skin.

I tried saying things to my father too, but only my bits of the picture were coloured. I remember thinking he must be keeping a big store of words and colours tucked deep inside, like a rainbow that nobody had ever been allowed to see.

Betrayal. A big word. It is some years later that I find out about this one.

I'm hardly ever invited to go with my elder brothers on one of their expeditions in the long summer holidays so this morning is a privilege. They're going down to the lake at the bottom of the long track that passes our house. They ask if I want to come along. Of course I do.

At three, my younger brother, Philip, is too young to go. I'm eight, and my two elder brothers, aged eleven and sixteen, are judged to be sensible enough.

My mother sits on her wooden stool in the kitchen. Several saucepans of water rattle and steam on the hob at her back. She's been picking beans and peas from the vegetable garden and now she's preparing to blanch them and bag them up for the freezer so she can feed us home-grown vegetables through the winter.

We stand soberly before her. She makes each of us promise not to go near the boathouse or the punt or the old rowing boat with holes in the bottom. These things are very dangerous and we could be badly hurt or even drowned.

We must be back for lunch. That gives us at least two hours.

The way down to the lake is dusty and narrow in summer. Bracken and nettles crowd in from the banks, forcing us to walk one behind the other so as not to be stung. My brothers have stashed crusts and penknives in the pockets of their khaki shorts. I have a supply of Opal Fruits in mine. We're free, our own guides and masters. If my brothers have made a plan, I'm not party to it.

The crowns of a stand of oak trees form a dark canopy over the drive. Here, on the left, is the Major's canoe high up on the bank. He brought it back from Africa in the 1930s, intending to float it on the lake, but the men carrying it couldn't get any further than this. So they put it down, right here. Whenever we walk here with my father, he points out that the canoe is a hollowed-out tree trunk and must have weighed more than six strong men could manage. The timber has bleached in places and rotted in others and tall grasses grow in the centre. We peer into the great hulk of the old boat and talk, as we always do, of how it was once paddled by a line of shiny black African men down the great grey-green, greasy Limpopo River, all set about with fever trees.

We walk on down the track as it bends around to the left. More trees overshadow us. Soon we're standing on the bridge that takes the track over the weir. To our left is the lake. To our right water gushes and foams from the sluices, leaving behind a tangle of twigs, half-rotted leaves and green slime. The drop is five or six feet into a round dark pool. Leaning on the metal rail, we study the way the currents move. David says the pool is so deep you'd never be able to reach the bottom, even with sub-aqua kit. I shiver, unwrapping an Opal Fruit inside my pocket.

But my brothers haven't come here to watch water swirl in double circles.

David is restless. *Come on, let's go. Last one there's a sissy.*

The path around the perimeter of the lake is muddy and invaded by brambles. Christopher goes on ahead, trampling them down as best he can. David walks close behind him, swiping at nettles with a whippy stick he's cut from a birch tree with his penknife. I bring up the rear.

We're heading straight for the boathouse. I can see it beyond a neck of water where a stream runs into the lake. I'm hot and confused. I keep thinking about what Mummy said, about how we mustn't go there. My brothers carry on, chanting a marching rhyme Nanny taught us: *Left, left, I had a good home but I left. Right, right, it served me jolly well right.*

I'm lagging behind, already the sissy, scared to say I want to go home, wishing I'd never come with them. Sick with fear, sick at the thought of the lies we'll have to tell.

My brothers know how to get into the locked boathouse, because they've done it before. David clambers on to Christopher's back, as though for a piggyback ride. Like this he can just reach the wired-up latch high on the plank door. He pulls his Swiss penknife out of his right pocket and uses the corkscrew to bend back the wire. As he drops onto the ground, the door swings open.

On one side of the little central jetty is the half-sunk punt, clearly of no real interest to my brothers. But the rowing boat on the other side sits proud in the water with two oars lying inside the hull. And several inches of water.

Needs bailing again, says David, fetching an old plastic bucket from a corner of the boathouse. I recognise it as one that Mummy used to keep in the laundry.

My brothers climb down into the boat, Christopher holding out a hand to me.

Don't you dare tell Mummy, David says, staring at me as he scoops up water with the bucket and empties it over the side. *Or you never come with us again. Don't tell anyone, okay?*

Something bad rises inside me as he says the words. *Don't. Tell. Anyone.* I've heard these words before.

Instead of taking Christopher's outstretched hand, I turn and run, letting the boathouse door bang behind me. Back along the lakeside path, faster than I've ever run. Dark trees and bright sunlight strobe above my head. I don't stop until I get to the weir. Then I look out across the moss-coloured lake. The rowing boat is heading for a tiny island in the middle of the water. I can see my brothers' heads and shoulders, arms moving oars.

Everything about the day has changed. As I puff and stumble up the track alone, I'm miserable and afraid. I've finished the last Opal Fruit by the time I halt at the Major's canoe. Perhaps Mummy will be outdoors and I can slip into the house without her seeing. I'll go up to my room and work things out.

In the end, I walk into the kitchen and she's there putting bright-green beans into bags. Her face is pink, her hair wavy from the steam.

She stops what she's doing, surprised to see me. *Back already? What on earth's the matter?*

And although I don't want to say anything, and although I hate the words as they come out, I tell her everything. In a rush. The boathouse. The rowing boat with holes. The bucket. How I ran away because I was frightened. How David and Christopher might be drowning, or sinking into the smelly mud. It's awful, awful. And

I tell her how I'm not meant to tell her. How they'll never want me with them again. How I'm bad. I should have kept this secret.

Don't tell them I told you. I'm sobbing now. *Please, please, please don't tell them.*

But in my stomach I'm sure they already know.

* * *

15 February, 2009

It's painful to realise that I've never really loved him and he's never really loved me. Nothing between us is remotely like love. I've wanted it to be, or rather I've wanted the clarity and truth of love. This sadness I feel isn't the sadness of a daughter whose father is dying; it's the sorrow of someone waking up to a gaping hole in her life. He's leaving and I want him to leave but, perversely, the thought of his leaving makes me sad – once he's gone I won't be able to cling to the fantasy that things can be put right.

I can't find the extra strength to deal with this. I dissolve when something small goes wrong and cry over nothing. Philip's patient but concerned. He *does* love me.

* * *

THE WORLD ACCORDING TO MY FATHER
6. ANGER

When it comes up inside you, this feeling of heat and energy, push it down for as long as you can.

75

Do not put a name to it, once a thing is named it really exists. (See *Denial*)

When it builds to a point of explosion, it is always surprising, even if anticipated. Like a volcanic eruption.

Anger is always right. Anger is power. Anger is purple and red.

Anger, at its maximum, overrides even sex.

* * *

20 February, 2009

Downpours again: blocked drains and flooding and power cuts. Clouds hang over the town and the Downs like a promise of an ending.

Yesterday I was at Dad's. I took him stuff he needed, got food in, collected prescriptions. Part of me asks the other part why I do it.

He never stops putting women down. He always finds ways of undermining women. Within three minutes of my being in the house, with his face right in mine, really angry, he says, *All those maddening ring tones on trains, they're always girls' phones, have you noticed?*

It makes me feel sick. I want to vanish. When he says these things about women I feel a burning heat in my stomach but my first reaction is to take the criticism, and push my own feelings under. My default setting is to be afraid of his anger.

* * *

Watching the old films, I see myself – as my father once saw me – through a lens. My way of looking at my father. His way of looking at me.

Ciné film, 1966

A broad wooden staircase, yellowed oak boards and banisters, overhead lighting from a bold 1960s brass chandelier. A brown-and-red patterned carpet up the centre of the stairs, polished brass stair rods. The girl, aged about eleven, stands and waits for some unknown, unknowable cue. It must have come, because she looks up and begins to walk slowly and steadily down towards the camera. She has shoulder-length blonde hair, fine and falling in waves. She is wearing an A-line black miniskirt, knee-length boots, and a blue roll-neck sweater. She moves nervously, her eyes lowered, her right hand stroking the banister as she descends, each foot hovering for a moment before making contact with the next step. Because of the perspective – the shot being taken from below – the girl's booted feet and calves seem bulky, forcing their way into the foreground with each move downwards. Even her thighs are too significant before they disappear into the shadow of her skirt. The top part of her diminishes abruptly, her eleven-year-old torso triangulated and shortened to alien proportions. Her eyes seem to be in a different realm from the rest of her body, close to a vanishing point at the top of her head. The girl never arrives at the bottom of the staircase. She stops a few steps before the last. The camera angle flattens out – the girl's shape looks almost normal. And she takes up most of the frame. Now, a quick surprised smile as she puts her left hand to her waist and readjusts the sweater where it needs to meet and overlap the skirt. Then a cut. Then a dust storm.

My father clicks off his ciné camera and puts it down on the hall table as I reach the bottom of the staircase. He stares at my face, the face that took me an hour to do. Unfamiliar fiddly work, an experiment of looking and altering. A mask. A first go at being a grownup.

What've you done, you silly girl? Go to your room, right now, and take off all that muck.

I turn and go back up the stairs. Feeling ashamed. He watches me. His camera eyes.

I close my bedroom door. I fill the wash-basin with hot water and lean over it so I have a full view of my face in the mirror above. Steam advances and retreats across the glass. I scrub at my eyes with a soapy flannel until the Mary Quant eye-shadow and navy-blue mascara blend into a semi-waterproof greyness around my stinging rims and lids. I wipe purple-brown lipstick onto tissue after tissue, leaving my lips dry and sore. And when my face is naked and blotched and I am very sure what humiliation feels like, I sit on my bed and hope that my mother will come and find me.

* * *

23 February, 2009

I'm at my desk at the top of the house, the ultraviolet lamp my only light. Blue winter, and I'm topping up the serotonin to fend off sadness. Wading my way through piles of paper.

Each phone call is a step nearer his death. I dread and anticipate the calls in equal measure. His death is the unknown. This strange love-hate I've known all my life *is* my relationship with him, it *is* how we have been. What will come after?

With him, unlike with my mother, I've had this brief and tantalising chance to listen to his way of wording things. All that listening with my mother was done much earlier, when I was too young. By the end of her life, in the care home, the only story she could tell was the one her feet spelled out as we danced around her room. All language had gone but she could still dance.

So our story continues, Dad's and mine, and will to the end, and beyond the end. We are bound together. The ties may slacken but they cannot disappear. I suppose I'll learn to deal with that. Nowadays we tend to communicate through his doctor – about his mood, his pain, how to help him adapt to having a carer. And whether he should still be driving. He's getting away with telling the doctor that he's okay to drive, that he's only taking the morphine at night. Meanwhile he's gulping morphine from the bottle all through the day and going out in the car whenever he wants.

There's so much unresolved stuff that he will never put to rest. It must be awful for him, flooded with terrifying waves of emotion and not knowing what to do with them. And yet, and yet, that's his own fault. Nothing to do with me.

For the first time in my life I'm witnessing his pain without feeling the need to help. I've carried his pain for so long and now I mustn't. I can't. I must let him carry his burden.

* * *

THE WORLD ACCORDING TO MY FATHER
7. LUGGAGE

Revelation is the best make of luggage.

Luggage must be lockable. Shame on anyone who leaves (full or empty) luggage locked but has not kept the key or a record of the combination number.

When not in use, luggage should be kept in the store-room.

Luggage left out waiting to be packed is perfectly acceptable. Luggage left out after unpacking is disorderly, even slovenly.

Nobody may borrow another person's luggage.

Packing luggage into the boot of a car is a highly-skilled activity. Women do not have spatial awareness so they can't do it.

An opened-up empty suitcase may be used as emergency extra bedding if cold prevents sleep.

* * *

28 February, 2009
He's fired three carers now. Lily's the latest – a gentle young woman of twenty-four who coped for ten days before he accused her of lying to him. He gave her thirty minutes to get ready to leave and told her he'd drive her to the station. She called me because she was worried he might really drive

when he was full of drugs. She knew he wasn't supposed to drive anymore.

Without a carer looking after him, his drug regime must be haywire, his body and mind raging beyond the cancer and the anger, throwing up memories of ancient pains he's ignored because he told himself they never existed. The poison has built up until he can no longer contain it. It overwhelms him.

The only way I can deal with this is to keep away, and anyway he won't accept my help, or concern or sympathy. He won't accept anything because he's fuelled by anger and aggression and denial. As he moves further from reality into fantasy, he thinks he isn't ill and he's sure he isn't dying. All he needs is a personal trainer and he'll soon be fit again and able to control his destiny. A man of such resource and power and importance must have what he wants.

On Saturday, I went to his house. He was wearing a thin cotton dressing gown with nothing underneath it except a urine bag strapped to his leg. He paced the room, shouting, *Damn you, bugger you.*

He didn't see me. I was invisible, a ghost in my own father's house, tiptoeing around in his fantasies, trespassing on his alternative reality.

If he sees me, he has to see what's happening to him. And he can't possibly do that.

* * *

THE WORLD ACCORDING TO MY FATHER
8. KNIVES

Keep your knives sharp and they will do a good job in skilled hands. Knives must be your servants.

Old knives are the best: a good carving knife is worn and has a concave, flexible blade that can be guided around the bones of a beef or lamb joint.

A carving knife should be sharpened on a honing steel or, if you don't have a steel, on another knife. Unless you are left-handed, the edge must be tested against your left thumb.

An axe should be sharpened professionally with a grinding stone. There is nothing worse than a blunt axe.

The best cut is a clean cut.

Sharpening knives is a man's job. Women are no good at it.

* * *

1 March, 2009
This new version of me becomes stronger as my father's illness gains momentum. I rattle my cage, louder and louder. I'm real. Watching Dad lose his reason, I quietly distil myself within my own body and hold fast to my truth while he shows his true self. Here in front of me is the man and the material he attempted to excise and hide when he sat in his study on

Sunday nights, cutting, cutting, splicing. Reconfiguring reality.

I can remember other times when I felt like this, when I've wished him dead – or at least I've wished him gone, vanished, continents away.

Feelings and thoughts from years and years ago are coming to the surface. I must allow those feelings to rise through me because my sanity depends on it. And I have to banish him. *I no longer want you to live. It's time. Please die now – even though I care about you and your leaving will cause me pain.*

I've needed to say this all my life and I haven't been able to: *Go away.* Instead, I've tried and tried to change the relationship and to make it work. I did this out of fear and out of need for the father I hoped he'd become.

But now I want to run free.

* * *

I imagine going west to Cornwall by the old familiar routes, arriving in that landscape as the sun begins to sink. I imagine walking out on a rugged peninsula in May or June and looking across to the stretch of coast we used to visit year after year from the late 1950s until the early 1970s.

This landscape is all sense and clarity. Along the top and lip of the cliff are magical seaside tones: thrifty pink and orchid mauve, blackthorn in white blossom, wild garlic, mustard gorse, meadowsweet and bluebells – colours I know from memory as well as imagination, colours of disappearance and desire. There are faded-denim blues. There are the early morning colours of sea caves and green foam bolting upwards and falling back into a cauldron sea. Shades of metal and smoke. My English colours. I must have absorbed them as I walked the coast or sat tucked under the cliff parapet with my father. That cliff was our silent meeting place, or at least the place where our words were drowned out by the voices of wind and sea and seabirds.

We have probably returned to the holiday house from the morning surf, rinsed off the salt and sand, changed into jeans and T-shirts and woollen jumpers.

He has said, *Shall we go to our favourite place?*
And I have said, *Yes Daddy…*

The sea spreads out before us like a great sheet of beaten pewter. There is the cliff edge, or at least the first edge, the one we will have to drop below to get to our hidden ledge.

It's only another minute's walk from here. I lick salt from my upper lip. My father sings, *He who would valiant be 'gainst all disaster, let him in constancy follow the Master.* His steps are slower and more careful as we approach the edge, then he slips me over his right shoulder and sets me to the ground a few feet short of the drop.

* * *

3 March, 2009
He's decided. He's going into a nursing home recommended by a good friend. A room has become available. He's met the matron and talked it through and he'll go in on Monday. It's on the ground floor with a view towards woods. It's all arranged and booked. I'm amazed.

* * *

There are no other tyre marks on the four inches of snow on his steep drive. I'm worried about the car getting stuck, so I park at the top and walk down.

I let myself in. This is the first time I've ever been inside his house when he's not here. I'm an intruder.

I find the extra things he wants, leave cash for the cleaner, pick up bills that need paying. Check all the windows and doors. Lock up again. Tramp back through the snow to the car with the boxes and bags. I drive to the nursing home with a strange cargo of incontinence pads, underwear, a few spare shirts, a warm jersey, the *Radio Times* and his list of medications which reads like an addict's shopping list.

The nursing home is a big Edwardian house. A finger sign points to 'Reception'. There are acres of red carpet. The house smells of fresh air spray, custard, gravy and hyacinths.

He's at lunch, a friendly nurse tells me, and shows me to his room to wait.

No 14. The number is in transfer letters on the door, and below the number, in black letters on a gold-foil background, his name as he must have wanted it: P. BEST.

Except for the notice, there are few signs that my father is living here, or that anyone's living here. Today's *Daily Telegraph* on the bedside table, a pile of books, a spectacle case. A green suitcase by the orthopaedic chair. I have to move the case to sit down. It's heavy. Full.

I sit in the adjustable chair and watch the door. The friendly nurse brings me tea and tells me they're monitoring his food and drink intake. He doesn't seem to be eating much. They've put all his medicines under lock and key because he was taking too much oral morphine and they couldn't keep track.

I wait. Ten, fifteen minutes perhaps, time drifting in this out-of-time place. From where I'm sitting, I can see across the red-carpeted passage straight into another room where a tiny gnarled person has nodded off in a chair identical to the one I'm sitting in. She's wrapped in a tartan rug like a child in the back of the car, her chin on her chest. She too is waiting.

Then I hear his voice, or rather a cracked, rasping version of it, approaching. *Who did you say was here to see me?* When he appears, he's on the arm of a different nurse. She delivers him and leaves us together. He sits down on the bed. When he realises it's me, he begins to cry.

This is the first time I've ever seen him cry and it's terrifying. A surge of maternal feeling threatens to overwhelm me but I manage to hold back my own tears. Today must be about containment. Seeing him here where he's looked after, I remind myself that I can walk away. *I am a separate person*, I tell myself in my head. *Time enough later for my own feelings.*

He spends the next half hour obsessing about his wallet, searching the bedside table and the chest of drawers. I offer to help but he doesn't hear me.

Where is it? I brought lots of money with me and I think I've lost it. 'Never lose sight of your money, my boy' – that's what my father used to say. But I can't hold onto money, never been able to. Oh bugger, where is that wallet, where is the fucking thing?

He shunts the green suitcase onto the bedside rug and fumbles it open, catching his fingernail on the zip. He curses again and again. I sit and watch as he first turns out the contents onto the floor, then puts everything back.

Eventually he finds the wallet in the back pocket of the trousers he's wearing. *Confucius say, 'You can't get wallet out of pocket while you're sitting down'.*

A pause.

They're watering down my morphine you know, selling the rest.

He stands up, pulls out the wallet, empties it and counts the ten-pound notes. He strokes them, sniffs them, rolls them up together, stuffs them into the wallet, then crams the wallet back into his trouser pocket.

I gaze down into the open suitcase, just as he does.

He seems to hear my question before I ask it. He's looking at me now. *They told me we had to get out, some kind of bomb scare. I packed in a helluva hurry. Five minutes to get ready.*

I think it's okay now, Dad.

I help him unpack all his stuff. I put shirts back on wire hangers, socks and underwear in the drawers, toothpaste and flannel in the en-suite bathroom where the mirror above the basin is at the correct height for a person sitting in a wheelchair.

* * *

THE WORLD ACCORDING TO MY FATHER
9. MONEY

Money is everything. If you have it you're a success, if you don't you're a failure.

Best of all is the money you've made yourself, preferably in large quantities. Earning it is acceptable, but making large amounts by investing it (or by investing other people's and taking a cut) is far better. If you can achieve both you're a double success.

If you've inherited money that's okay, but not great, unless you've turned your inheritance into something much bigger.

Women with money are a different thing, undeniably attractive and admirable at one level, disturbing at another. Women may inherit money but they should not earn it because that makes them threatening.

People who work part-time (mostly women) should not draw a salary. They're too unreliable.

A man should always have more money than the woman he associates most closely with, and he should also decide how her money is invested and spent.

Women who pay with large amounts of cash are vulgar, especially in supermarkets or restaurants.

Money makes the best gift at birthdays and Christmas (see *Gifts*). The recipient should always thank you for it at least twice.

Money should only be spent on certain things: cars, ski holidays, cruises, smoked salmon, a satellite dish or a state-of-the-art TV. Otherwise money should be put to work so that it grows and becomes Capital.

You must never spend Capital, only the income from it, which is then money again. It's like the water cycle.

* * *

10 March, 2009

Yesterday his pain poured out, smothering and infecting me. I took it away with me.

He was okay again last night. I know because I called the duty nurse when I got home. He was restful and ate a good dinner.

This morning it's raining. I'm exhausted. I daren't call the nursing home, daren't find out how he is today. Here in my own house I can distance myself a bit from his pain.

12 March, 2009

He fights on. Six messages on my answerphone when I got in this evening.

He wants to leave the nursing home and go home. Wants me to fix it. He tells me again that the nurses are watering down his morphine and selling the spare bottles.

He rants and raves. He tells me I'm a bad daughter. I'm neglecting him. *You are wretched. You don't care, you little shit.*

I've been thinking about my mother, about what she might do now if she were still alive.

* * *

My mother did wonderful things with eggs and butter and cream. She was the cholesterol queen.

She used to tell me how she went to Ireland with my father just after the War and drank fresh farm cream from the bottle. She sat in the lush grass in her wool skirt and swigged it down. It was such a luxury after the deprivations of the wartime diet, she said, that she couldn't help herself. Apparently my father laughed.

When we were children, my mother baked at least twice a week. All the cakes and puddings were made with free-range eggs and full-cream milk. And with butter, unless she had run out or couldn't get it, when she would substitute Stork margarine.

I help by creaming the butter in a big mixing bowl with a wooden spoon until it's glossy and pale. Together we weigh out the caster sugar and flour. We break the eggs and beat them in a smaller bowl.

My mother's standard Victoria sponge is a fine piece of work. I love the delight of varying the mix for orange or lemon cake, chocolate or coffee cake. We always bake it in a single tin. My mother turns it out and lets it cool before slicing it horizontally with a carving knife into two perfectly equal parts. I cream more butter for the butter icing to go in the sandwich while she weighs the icing sugar and measures the water for the glacé icing we'll pour on top. Then there are the bright red glacé cherries, or the pieces of sugary orange or lemon jelly, or the chocolate buttons, depending on the flavour of the cake.

Apart from the variations on Victoria sponge, there are other cakes that come and go from my mother's repertoire. Rich Plain Cake, which my Aunt Auriol introduces, has an ingredients list to rival some of Mrs Beeton's – eight eggs, butter in eye-watering quantities, mountains of sugar and about a pound of ground almonds. We make this cake before long car journeys. To this day, I can't taste almonds without seeing my mother wrapping the Rich Plain Cake in two layers of foil and lowering it ceremonially into a deep Tupperware Cake Taker, my father unpacking and repacking the intricately-figured boot of his Jaguar to accommodate it. Thin slices provide rich, nutritious snacks for two adults and four children all the way to Basel, Brittany or Bodmin.

A latecomer to the range of cakes in our household is one known as a fatless sponge. Perhaps it's my mother's concession to cutting down a little on saturated fats when these first fall under suspicion in the 1970s. This slightly rubbery cake consists only of eggs, flour, a little sugar and milk. It is tasteless, but this defect is remedied by what is done after the baking. My mother sandwiches the two layers of the cake together with whipped double cream studded with sugared strawberries. If she can lay her hands on clotted cream she uses this instead.

If all these cakes provide the weekly worship, the liturgy, in our kitchen, it is what my mother does with eggs that supplies the mystery. Eggs are the embodiment of her domestic magic. She's a genius with them.

She never gets shell in the broken egg, the yolks don't burst when she separates yolk from white, nothing she makes ever curdles. Her home-made custard is smooth and rich, shiny as newly-washed hair in the sun. Her poached, fried, baked eggs, even boiled eggs all have the hallmark of perfection. She makes omelettes in a kind of dream state, and for special occasions she produces a soufflé omelette to die for, finished under the grill, puffed up and proud, golden to the eye and light on the palate.

Once I'm considered old enough, at about ten, to share responsibility for something so sophisticated, we experiment with new types of soufflé. We make spinach and chard soufflé, smoked salmon soufflé, and we serve them with salad from the garden. My mother and I enjoy them much more than the others. Eggs have become a shared passion.

As I grew up and away, I took my mother's cookery with me, going into adulthood with a preference for baking, egg-based sauces, quiches and omelettes. I adapted a few recipes to make them my own while others remained unaltered. And some treats I ate only in her kitchen when I visited at weekends, Easter or Christmas. The most delicious were her pancakes.

It wasn't until many years after her death that I dared revisit the pancake, my mother's most assured creation, and then it was with a sense of trespass that I went out and bought the right kind of aluminium pan, found a recipe that approximated to how I remembered hers, and began to practise.

* * *

23 March, 2009
Done. The miracle! He's home with the new carer, Annabel, who comes highly recommended by friends and with a chance gap in her schedule. She's a strong angel or Mary Poppins or both. The answer to my prayers.

If he accepts her and if she can cope with him, she'll look after him at home until he dies. She'll help him live the end of his life with the appropriate medical support. He needs to allow her to do that. Please, oh please. I feel so relieved I can't even cry. I want to sleep for a week.

I am spending part of my life living his life and his death. Another part is spent writing all this. Because I must. Because somehow it helps.

I dare to imagine life after death, my life after his death. Excitement is gradually replacing fear. I'm approaching the end of the story of 'him and me'. And perhaps one day I'll be able to speak of all these things.

* * *

My father despised his stepmother. Whenever he spoke of Mater, the hatred on his face was appalling and fascinating.

Because of this deep-seated enmity, and because my grandfather had died in the early 1940s leaving Mater a widow, my father had no need to see her. My brothers and I never met her. The horror stories and a few family photographs were all we knew of her.

There was only one point of contact between Mater and our family. Every year, just before Easter, a large brown paper parcel would arrive from Fortnum & Mason. My father knew what it contained, as did my mother, so I'm not sure why they opened it, since my father always disposed of the contents immediately.

However, each year the layers of packaging were carefully removed to expose a fruitcake decorated with a circle of marzipan balls and wrapped in cellophane. There was always a printed card that said, 'With good wishes to you all, Mater'. Every year my father folded up the brown paper and put it away in the utility cupboard. Then he dropped the Simnel cake and the card into the kitchen bin, washed his hands and got on with something else, cursing *that abominable woman.*

It was the twenty-eighth of March, precisely thirty-seven years after his mother's death, that my father returned from work and took a telephone call from his sister telling him that Mater had died a few hours earlier.

His face relaxed. I noticed the way he stood up straighter, as if a weight had been lifted off his shoulders. He even grew merry as the evening went on and there was a sense of relief and lightness around the table.

After supper, my mother gave him a big hug and said, *That's the end of that story then. Mater's gone to meet her maker!*

That year, Easter Sunday fell on April the tenth. The preceding Wednesday, my mother and I were clearing up breakfast when the postman rang the doorbell. My mother brought in the large brown parcel.

It's called a standing order, my mother said, with a dry laugh. *Best to leave it for your father to deal with.*

She placed the parcel on the kitchen table where it sat until evening.

When he got home, my father silently picked up the parcel and took it straight out to the shed where the big metal bins were kept. I heard a clang as he took off the bin lid and another clang as he replaced it. He must have dropped the entire parcel in. Back inside, he washed his hands at the kitchen sink and poured himself a generous Scotch.

* * *

29 March, 2009
My parents' wedding anniversary.

It's already many weeks since I first felt drained of energy. He keeps going, confounding everyone, swinging between energetic denial of his illness and intense disappointment and sadness. This business of living, the work of hanging on, is a full-time job for him. And it needs a network of supporters to dress the dummies, paint the sets and move the props.

Back in his own house, he's looked after superbly by Annabel, who metes out his pills, dresses his wounds, runs errands, prepares his favourite foods, sees to his whims, leaves him when he wants to be alone. She consoles the inconsolable, avoids the denied. She is there for him when he wants her.

Is he finally the child he couldn't be? And is she the mother, answering his every physical need, asking his friends around to play, washing him and putting him to bed? Explaining to him why he feels like he feels. Mopping the tears he's learning to produce.

Then there are the doctors and community nurses. There are Macmillan advisors. Women to clean his house and look after the garden.

And me. I'm stuck in the waiting room again.

* * *

```
Transcript:
I was in London on leave. I picked up Heather
at her parents' flat at Queensgate Gardens, in
a taxi, and so I didn't really see her, all I
could do was smell her. She smelled absolutely
wonderful. So that was my first impression of
her. I couldn't see her.
```

* * *

After that blind date in March 1945, my parents seem to have had a whirlwind romance spanning my father's short leave. But he had to go back to sea, and my mother – who was beautiful and popular – was left to untangle the threads of several other relationships. They married two years later, on the twenty-ninth of March 1947.

My father had been recruited into the Royal Naval Volunteer Reserve in 1941 and served until 1946, reaching the rank of Lieutenant. When the War ended, he wanted a career in the regular Navy as opposed to 'the wavy navy' but he wasn't accepted so he had to think about what to do in Civvy Street to support himself and my mother and their life together.

Following a brief and painful stint working in an accountancy office, my father met a family friend who offered to introduce him to a contact in the paper industry. This resulted in him joining Wiggins Teape in 1946 on an accelerated trainee programme. He climbed steadily through the ranks, eventually becoming Managing Director in 1976. Soon after that, he was invited onto the main board of the new parent company, British American Tobacco. He was a well-respected 'Captain of Industry' in the 1970s and beyond, up to his retirement in 1984.

Judging from how he talked about it at home, my father seldom enjoyed his work. He complained about his colleagues, about the politics and the posturing. Corporate financial responsibilities burdened him and I remember my mother soothing him over evening drinks when he came home from the office. He appeared to enjoy the travelling that went with the senior roles after promotion from his job as Mill Manager at Dartford in 1962. From the early 1960s onwards, he was often away on business trips to Europe, India, Brazil, Argentina, the USA and Australia. Once or twice a year my mother had the company's blessing to go with him.

It seems that my father was almost universally liked, respected and admired by friends and colleagues all over the world as well as at home in the UK.

Whenever accounts of child sex abuse emerge in the press, people say, *But surely not him, he always seemed so normal / kind / good / respectable / loving.* We want to believe that abusers are monsters but generally they look and behave like responsible people. It is this invisibility, this duality, which makes them dangerous. They're amongst us but we can't spot them. They tend to be clever, devious and good at getting what they want – mainly our trust.

Instead of achieving a successful career as a senior executive followed by retirement on a large pension, my father should have gone to prison in his early forties after being found guilty of sexually abusing his daughter. I wonder what would have become of him. Of us.

* * *

THE WORLD ACCORDING TO MY FATHER
10. PARTIES

Invitations should be sent out on stiff white cards.

One must prepare very thoroughly when giving a party. Particular attention should be paid to the drinks supply. Food is less important. A host will be judged on the quantity as well as the quality of the wine and other drinks on offer.

Informal parties resemble formal parties in every respect except for the dress code.

No party guest may enter the kitchen or other backstage areas of the house where food or drink are being prepared or where there might be visible untidiness or signs of normal everyday life.

For pre-lunch drinks parties, the ice must be in the ice bucket at least half an hour before the guests are due. Likewise glasses must be arranged in neat lines on trays, and nuts and crisps should be put out in bowls well in advance.

It is a fact of entertaining that the first guest to arrive will always be the one you least want to spend time with, but as the host you must try to make them feel as welcome as possible.

The host's acute stress before the party is in precise energetic balance with the amount of drink that will need to be consumed by that host before relaxation is achieved.

Once the last guest has departed, the real party may begin. But before this can happen, all the used glasses and cocktail sticks must be gathered up and put in the kitchen so that the house is purged of all signs that guests have been there.

Parties are not for fun, they are for paying off debts. They are part of the complex social contract.

* * *

Ciné film, 1962. The girl's 7th birthday, Broomfields

Children are ranged across a lawn. Boys in knee-length shorts and collared shirts and lace-up shoes. Girls in pretty dresses – smocked, sashed, pleated – their hair tied in bows or held back with Alice bands. The children are all facing in the same direction, perhaps focused on the same thing. A woman is to the right of shot, just visible in a mid-calf-length skirt, her back turned to the children, her right arm raised, the children running towards her. When she drops her arm, the children freeze. Then she turns around, points to one or two of those who are wobbling in their frozen positions. They run back, to start again. The woman raises her arm, the children rush forward, freezing again when the arm comes down. Each time the children stop, the camera pans over to the woman, then back across the lawn with its small figures. Grandmother's Footsteps. There she is in the middle of the shot: the girl. The camera stays on her as she freezes. Her seventh birthday party is happening all around her. Cut. Some of the same children sit in a circle. A large parcel is being passed around. Occasionally the unheard music must be halted because a child unwraps a layer of brown paper. From outside the circle, the woman reaches her hand in to receive each piece of discarded wrapping. The passing and unwrapping gets quicker until eventually the parcel reaches the girl. She waits with it in her lap. The woman bends over her and helps her tear off the last layer of paper. She is left holding what looks like a real baby, but it must be a baby doll.

* * *

Our home was always full of paper. In my father's study there were stacked boxes of headed notepaper in Wedgewood blue, cream or ivory. The paper was always Wiggins Teape's Conqueror (when I come across this brand I still like to hold the sheet up to the light and study the watermark), and there were more boxes full of matching Conqueror envelopes, and other boxes full of plain white invitation cards, and yet others containing Conqueror postcards with my parents' names and address at the top.

Every time we moved house, which was quite often, another batch of headed stationery was ordered and delivered, and the stationery from the previous home was officially demoted and released as scrap paper, suitable for drafting homework or lists. So we made our notes and jottings on fine paper, and to this day I find it almost impossible to write even a shopping list on poor-quality paper.

In addition to all the smart stationery, there were plenty of notepads from my father's trips and conferences as well as samples of interesting new products – like the early prototypes for invoice pads when NCR (No Carbon Required) paper was pioneered by Wiggins Teape. I recall the novelty of writing on the top sheet and seeing how the script magically went through to the second and third sheets.

Because we lived with so much paper, and because my father often talked at mealtimes about the manufacturing processes and the many things that could go wrong, we children picked up a working knowledge of papermaking. We knew the ingredients of various papers, the difference between a laid paper and a bond, the importance of the direction of the paper's grain, and the uses of coated papers. Three of us went on to be involved with paper in different ways: Christopher spent some time working in the manufacturing side of the industry, David made his first career in marketing paper, and I became a bookbinder and conservator, later moving across to bookselling and publishing. Only Philip, the youngest, more or less escaped the pull of my father's material, although as a banker and fund manager I suppose, in his way, he's been as close to paper as any of us.

* * *

Here's another of the secrets. For a long time I felt deeply ashamed of it. Even now, I have an ineradicable sense that I should have been able to say No. But that's not how it works. The rule of terror, the possession and the power dictate what happens and they remove choice and free will. Shame, and the fallout from the self-loathing that shame causes, are darkly persistent.

It is always afternoon. You are lying on your back on your bed. No clothes on, legs spread, skin of your thighs smooth against the strawberry-pink candlewick counterpane your grandmother gave you the day you were seven. She told you later how she crept into your room and laid it out on your bed before you woke that morning so you'd find it there, the first thing you saw when you opened your eyes on your birthday. Exactly the colour you'd asked for.

He's on the other side of the room. He's looking out of the window, facing away, hands behind his back. Just so, every time. He's giving orders. It's a game. Like Simon Says.

He tells you that if you do it right, he won't turn around. You can be private. But if you don't do everything the way he wants you to, and if you don't say exactly what he tells you to say, he'll know. He has eyes in the back of his head, sharp eyes especially for you.

You should know that by now, he says.

When you disobey or when you don't speak up, he comes over to where you are. He's silent. Not smiling. You can tell there's no smile even when you can't see his face. But sometimes he's laughing.

He kneels down on the floor by the bed, strokes the insides of your legs and pinches your thighs. Pushes fingers inside. Jab, jab, jab. You're rigid with knowing and not knowing what will happen next. He tells you again what he'll do if you're bad and don't obey him.

Eyes in the back of his head.

Secrets. Hard heavy things that have long been packed carefully in layers of silence. The secrets have become more and more closed, the wrapping more minutely folded and sealed. Promises and silences, known and kept.

At first, and for years, the silence was wrapped so tight around the secrets that they couldn't be seen or heard at all, not by me and certainly not by anyone else. This silence enclosing the secrets used to be my resting place. Blank and calm and numb and knowing no words. Simply being.

It was much later that I realised that each locked-away secret held a lost part of myself. Imagine a piece of music with gaps in the melody where the notes have been rubbed out. I wanted to collect the missing notes. Every time I managed to access a bad memory, I found a part of myself and could retrieve it. Together, the notes of the secrets joined up into music I wanted to hear. Music I could hear quite clearly. Full of pain and full of beauty and strangeness, this music surprises and compels me.

And the remaining silences, the gaps and missing notes that can never be found? These are part of the music. Instead of imagining my life as a scatter of separate bits and pieces, I can summon the notes and the gaps and begin to see how they link together.

I no longer want to listen to the music by myself, in my head. I want to sing that music out loud. It's strange and terrible, but it's real and true.

* * *

20 April, 2009

I've waited a long time for my father. I'm still waiting for him to come back to me. Most of all, in this spring space near the end of his life, I'm waiting for him to say things. I want him to admit what he did to me. I want to understand how and why, as much as I can, before he dies.

I'm having panic attacks in the night. Most nights. And dreams that repeat. I find myself in locked sunlit rooms with white sheets at the windows. So quiet these rooms, and with a special quality of emptiness that holds the fact that they've been full of people. But my family's gone, all gone, and I feel free and alone but locked in. When I fall asleep again, I find myself in another such room, always sensing my family has just left. Bright sunlight, the door locked.

My fear is of being annihilated by and in his death. I have been, still am, so bound to him.

I try to be in the dream room without worrying about working it out. I try to be there, safe and sunlit, with the voices retreating down the passage and the white sheets at the window.

* * *

I hate lists of symptoms. I hate having to admit that these things apply to me.

The fallout is at least as bad as the abuse itself. The effects on my relationships with others. The effects on my mental and emotional health and on my physical strength. The problems to overcome. The hard work to be done. The way it has to be done. That's a list already.

* * *

LIST ONE
Scripts in Incestuous Families (adapted from David Calof)

After abuse, systems of denial, unconscious rules, flawed family narratives and secrets are almost universal. Without treatment and recovery, the fallout from abuse in dysfunctional families continues well into adulthood. Here are some of the assumptions underlying these family behaviours:

1. Deny. The injunction to deny one's actual experience is the crux of the matter: do not think, see, hear, feel, reflect or question your experience. Accept the impossible.
2. Be loyal. You must protect the family, keep the secrets, obey. You must not fight back, disagree or get angry.
3. Don't have needs of your own.
4. Accept that love means being hurt or used.
5. Don't ask for help.
6. Don't show pain. Instead you will have somatic manifestations and complaints. You may be prone to self-injury and mutilation.
7. Don't be a child. There is no potential for innocent, curious

developmental exploration. Don't make mistakes. Be responsible for everyone else.

8.   It is your fault. You are bad, immoral, to blame. This will be manifest as scapegoating.
9.   You are responsible for others' behaviours. They are not responsible for their own behaviour. You must help them.
10. Stay in control of yourself and those around you. This may lead to hyper-arousal and hyper-vigilance.
11. Don't reflect, question or process.
12. Understand that denial and dissociation are fundamental principles of family life.

* * *

10 May, 2009
Yesterday's operation to adjust Dad's stent was cancelled. His clotting rate was too abnormal for surgery, he might have bled to death. He seemed to think that was okay.

I don't care, it's time I went. That could be quite a good option.
I said, *Not for the surgeon and theatre staff.*

The op's now rearranged for Tuesday. I called his doctor to ask if this procedure is really a good idea. She says it should make him more comfortable.

Another week of waiting.

13 May, 2009
I had a nightmare last night that was still with me when I woke. I was hyperventilating, in physical trauma. I surfaced enough to know it was about my father. Within seconds I must have been asleep again.

This morning Philip asked me how I slept.

Badly, I said. *I had a terrible nightmare.*

He said, *I know. I was quite worried. I wondered if I ought to wake you.*

I wish I could recall what was happening but it's just out of reach. Oh, how I wish I had it. It's the not knowing which is so difficult. The gaps. The feeling of being frozen.

Today I feel stunned, sick and tired, like I have a bad hangover.

* * *

LIST TWO
Psychiatric Symptoms Associated with Childhood Abuse (adapted from J. Douglas Bremner)

PTSD

   Nightmares
   Flashbacks
   Memory and concentration problems
   Hyperarousal
   Hypervigilance
   Intrusive memories
   Avoidance
   Abnormal startle responses
   Feeling worse when reminded of trauma

Dissociative

   Out-of-body experiences
   Amnesia
   Fragmented sense of self and identity

Anxiety
Panic attacks
Claustrophobia

* * *

Transcript:

We spent some time at the end of the War in
the Greek Islands. That was a very pleasant
interlude where nothing very much happened. Pretty
soon after that we were told to go home and so
we made our way from Greece back via Malta again.
I hadn't got a watch-keeping certificate, not
having been on a big ship long enough. But I
used to keep a watch and it was fun to feel
you were driving this enormous boat. Anyway we
were on our way home and suddenly a great fog
came down. Aurora's radar was not very good and
so at nights it was a bit alarming, you were
relying on sounds of foghorns and that sort of
thing. And we were going quite fast, probably
over twenty knots in this thick fog, and I
thought, I don't like this very much. The Captain
had a sea cabin which was just behind the bridge,
so I stuck my head round the corner and said,
Can I have a word with you Sir? He said, What's
the problem, Patrick? And I said, Well have a
look — thick fog. We talked for a bit about
when we were supposed to arrive in Portsmouth
and he eventually said to me, Well I'm not going

to be late, my wife will be there and I intend
to be on time so I suggest you keep going. And
I said, Not perhaps with a reduced speed Sir?
And he said, No, keep going. So sure enough we
did arrive more or less on time as I recall and
tied up in Portsmouth Harbour and Heather arrived
in a car to meet me.

* * *

LIST THREE
Problems my father's abuse caused for me

Unreasonable fear of things being put inside my body.
Unreasonable fear of the dentist, amounting at times to phobia.
Recurrent bouts of cystitis throughout my childhood.
Anxiety and panic attacks at times of acute stress.
Physical flashbacks and terrors.
Insomnia.
Serious unease about being in small rooms and cramped spaces.
The persistent default belief that my main purpose in life is to
    give other people pleasure.
Intermittent prosopagnosia (face blindness) especially when under
    stress.
Fear of intimate relationships and sex.
Fear of having to be at a certain place at a certain time.
Inexplicable feelings of guilt and shame.
Tendency to be over-obedient and too keen to please.
Sense of being unclean.
Periodic persistent anger and sadness.

Periods of depression.
Mysterious illnesses.
Memory problems.
Numbness.

* * *

Transcript:

It must have been early 1946 I came back to
Portsmouth. That was the end of the War for
me, and the last I saw of the ship. We were
paid off and actually Aurora was going to the
Chinese Navy and we had the ship full of men
putting up lists and notices in Chinese all
over the place saying Push this button or
Pull here or This box contains. I was then
in Civvy Street. They gave me a bowler hat
and a suit. I started trying to find a job.
I worked for a while for Alexander Cowan at
their offices in Upper Thames Street and the
job consisted of copying out invoices by hand
at a stand-up desk with a quill, well not
quite a quill but a steel pen. I stuck this
for a few weeks for some terrible amount of
money, it was a few quid a week — less than
I was getting as a Lieutenant in the Navy.
Then I went to the Scotsman who ran the place
and I said, Tell me Sir what are the prospects
of promotion out of this job? And he said,
Well laddie they're not very good. So I said,

```
If that's the case I think I'm going. Soon
after that I joined Wiggins Teape as a trainee
papermaker.
```

* * *

LIST FOUR
Features I have developed as a reaction and in compensation

Good at dissociation; I can 'leave' my body.
I make use of wakeful night hours for thinking and writing.
I've learned to overcome some kinds of fear and I cope with
    others.
Well-developed (at times over-developed) powers of empathy.
Great appreciation of solitude.
Intense powers of observation and concentration.
Resilience.
A gift for keeping secrets.
A facility for living in the present.
An ability to exist simultaneously in two separate modes.

* * *

THE WORLD ACCORDING TO MY FATHER
11. LISTS

Means of power and control over the vagaries of the universe.

Source of accomplishment, satisfaction, pride.

'To Do' lists should be made regularly, checked often and items crossed off when completed.

A person must never be without a list.

A missing list must be found.

* * *

There's an unravelling through the summer. A slow unveiling.

I wait for my chance to open the conversation we've never had. I want him to admit that he knows what he did. I want him to tell me he's sorry. This is the minimum I need to cope with continuing to live after he dies.

The nights before my visits to him, I lie awake, trying to think how to probe the subject. How to help him open the door. I wonder if I should be calm and quiet so that he knows I care about how the secrets are told. I am ready to play it carefully. I want to help myself heal.

A few times he's seemed ready to talk, almost welcoming the chance. He reaches for the key, raises it to the lock. Enough for me to think, *It's going to happen.* But he puts the key back in his pocket and turns away.

I can't insist. I haven't the courage. Despite my own needs rising in me, I feel I must respect his needs and wait for him to talk. It's the only way I can love him, and I need so badly to be able to love him in some way. Or at least that's how it feels. I'm caught in the bind.

* * *

Ciné film, 1964

The girl has short hair. She is wearing a blue, Chinese-style jacket and baggy blue trousers. There's a pink flower in her hair. She and her younger brother are side by side, and she's holding his hand. They both stand very still, expressionless, against a backdrop of windblown rhododendrons, the camera's eye moving across them before coming to rest on an expanse of bluebells and red polyanthus around a garden shed. The shot pulls quickly back to the two children. They both smile now, the same frozen smile, starting at the same moment. Their hands are still linked. There's a tilt and wobble, the camera dips to take in the photographer's brown leather shoes, and next to them, lying face down on the ground, two of the girl's dolls. One of the brown leather shoes moves the dolls to the side with a sharp, jerking action and the camera zooms in on a number of wasps circling a hole in the ground. The film fades to pink and grey dust, and at last the familiar blackness.

* * *

16 May, 2009

Time's running out. Time to think of our relationship finishing. To follow the shared track as far as it goes. It will never truly end, of course. I'll go on working things out, piecing the parts of myself back together.

Dad's friend Lucia called me yesterday. She'd recently got back from a long trip to visit family in the USA and on return she went to see Dad, to catch up with him. She told me that Dad was a bit drunk and said things about his stepmother, about my mother and about me.

Weird, odd things and his face changed when he spoke about them, Lucia told me.

She wouldn't say more.

I began to shake. *I'll need to call you back so that I can ask you about these things.*

When I put the phone down I went into a long panic attack, couldn't breathe properly, sweating, heart thumping. What secrets were delivered to the wrong ears when I had waited all this time for him to talk?

I feel betrayed.

It's as though he's bleeding into me, but I can't contain the blood – it's going to leak out and destroy everything. I'm close to the edge. The whole day has been dangerous. I'm in terrible pain. I can't tell his pain from mine.

He phoned this afternoon, told me he's seeing people everywhere – rooms full of them at night, figures in the corners of the room in the daytime. They creep in and out of the bushes in his garden and look through his windows after dark.

Serves him right.

17 May, 2009
I called Lucia back but she refused to say more. She told me it was private, between her and him, and she's determined to keep it that way.

* * *

Ciné film, 1965
Who is behind the camera? Not the man, this time. He is playing croquet on a smooth lawn, with the girl. The scene moves jerkily

from one hoop to another as the two players progress around
the course. The man takes his shots seriously, focusing intently,
lining up ball and hoop. He plays three shots, one after another,
each winning him the next. At last he hands the mallet to the girl
who swings it but misses the ball.

* * *

18 May, 2009
Today I drove there, stayed a couple of hours, drove back.
The stairlift was fitted. After much cursing at the man fitting
it, Dad was finally pleased. He went up and down eight or
nine times to demonstrate, although he then got cross with
it because it was too slow. *If there were a sports version, I'd
have paid extra for it!*

Later he was alternately voluble and tearful. We didn't
manage a sensible conversation. He was mostly complaining
about Annabel, asking when she'd leave because he couldn't
stand her.

Then he started on me, wanting to know when I'd let him
drive again.

*It's not possible now Dad, you're taking too many drugs to be safe
on the road.*

You little shit! he said, right in my face.

Tides of emotion flow through me when he looks at me like
that. Shame, guilt, disgust, fear of what next. The child in me
wants to hide.

You don't rule my life, he said.

Then he told me he couldn't have a woman living in the house
and not have a sexual relationship with her. He thought he might

marry Mary (in her eighties and with cancer) so she could move in and be his wife and carer, and then Annabel could leave because it's too difficult not having sex with Annabel.

I said, *Don't you think it's a bit late for another relationship?*

I made tea and he wanted to talk about the afterlife.

Do you believe there's an afterlife?

Perhaps the afterlife is about being safe and going home, I suggested.

He thought for a moment. *I never had a real home, no mother providing a home.*

He liked the idea of being safe. I think his only home has been himself. I think he's increasingly comfortable with this mad, exaggerated version of himself, confabulating, telling people whoppers on the phone, such as, *I'm going to get a personal trainer, going to start running again*, when he can't even walk across the room.

In the first half hour, he took thirty millilitres of oral morphine. Why does he always take so much morphine when I'm there?

He takes the morphine and some of my pain dulls too. We drift together into a false silence.

* * *

Transcript:
And my next promotion of course, about 1958, was as Mill Manager so I was allowed to live in the Mill House which was Broomfields, a much bigger place up the road in the same area. I had to live close to the Mill so I could go

down there when it caught fire, that sort of thing, which happened quite often actually.

* * *

Ciné film, 1960
Broomfields. Pan across the mock-Tudor front of a large house, then the garden, full of the crude primary colours of indistinguishable flowers. Suddenly a troupe of girls dance out from behind a mass of tall shrubs. The older girls, perhaps twelve and thirteen, are dressed in white tutus and wear their hair like Margot Fonteyn. They perform, curtsy, exit. Then come younger dancers, dressed in kimonos, holding ribbons. The girl is one of them, her fair hair half-tied in a knot at the back of her head. She moves more or less in unison with the other kimono girls, looking sideways now and then to check she is in step with them. They too curtsy, and run off on tiptoes. Cut. The same panning shot of the house, then the garden, this time monochrome. It is snowing heavily. The trees and shrubs are laden. Two boys ride their bikes across the garden and deliberately ditch them in the snow.

* * *

The first home I can remember is that house in Dartford. Broomfields, the one my parents moved to after I was born.

The centre of the house was oak-panelled and dimly lit. I would stand at the bottom of the stairs, surrounded by doors and wondering which one to open. The handles were all too high but by standing on tiptoe and reaching up with both hands, linking them over the handle and hanging my five years of weight, I could usually open any door I wanted.

The downstairs is clear in my mind with its three important rooms.

The kitchen, full of busyness, washing, cooking and chatter, a place inhabited by aproned women (my grandmother, my mother, Nanny) and smelling of bacon, apples, Lux soap flakes. The drawing room, smelling of a mixture of cigarettes and vase flowers and my mother's Arpège perfume. And the dining room with its mysterious brown scents of floor polish and gravy.

On Saturday mornings, after breakfast, a large woman with thick-lensed spectacles and brown leather shoes would ring the front doorbell. My mother let her in, called my two elder brothers and hushed them into the dining room where the woman was waiting for them, unpacking her canvas bag onto the shiny table. I thought of her as a kind of magician or good witch.

I stayed long enough to see the tutor sit down at the head of the table where my father sat on Sundays and at Christmas, and position one boy either side of her. I'd be pulled away then, and my mother would close the door on the beginning of the Latin lesson. The boys would be busy for an hour and I was to play on my own. I imagined them breathing Latin, repeating after the teacher those unfamiliar flat sounds in strange incantations and then writing down the words with their soft pencils. It was a wonderful ritual from which I was excluded and I longed to join them in the sombre room with the lined Exercise Books and the chanting.

Now, the three rooms are weighted equally in my consciousness. But when I was small, the dining room attracted me most, with

117

its forbidden books, its never-ending promise of roast lunches, and silent emptiness the rest of the time.

Upstairs, the house was a different country. An oak staircase rose grandly from the dark hall into a theatre of light. All the bedrooms opened off one long passage, at the end of which my grandmother, my mother's mother, had two rooms. Her own domain within ours.

She emerged frequently, and because she trod softly in her carpet slippers I never heard her coming. She would drift into proximity, unsummoned, in billowing ankle-length skirts, her grey hair pinned in marcel waves against a round head. She was always smiling, or so it seemed to me.

Granny came from her rooms to help my mother bathe or dress or feed us. In the evenings, she would read to us. Sometimes she went downstairs, sat at the piano, and sang while she played. Hebridean songs, mostly. *Ca' the Yowes* was her favourite. She had trained at the Guildhall School of Music at the end of the first decade of the twentieth century, under Gustave Garcia. He told her she would never have a singing career if she married. She married almost straightaway, in 1913, and went to Assam as a tea planter's wife. For years she played the piano and sang to herself.

* * *

Ciné film, 1961
Broomfields in winter, under about eight inches of snow. The front of the house, its leaded lights darkly reflective. Slow left to right shots of walls and trees, so the photographer can show the thickness of the snow. The girl walks towards the camera, until

her face fills the frame. She is wearing a brown wool hat pulled down over her ears. She lifts her right arm – she is holding a snowball in her red-gloved hand. She smiles, puts the snowball to her mouth and begins to eat it.

* * *

25 May, 2009

Yesterday when I went to see Dad, Freddie came with me. At thirteen, he shows remarkable maturity and compassion. But it was an awful encounter. We hadn't been in the house five minutes before Dad was demonstrating to Freddie something he used to show me as a child.

The movements are horribly familiar, the way he manipulates one arm with the other, twisting his left forearm around with his right until it stands up erect. Slow, deliberate, exaggerated actions. Then he nips his right elbow with the fingers of his left hand, simultaneously opening and closing the right fingers and thumb like a mouth moving. All the time, the look on his face is the same as when he used to beckon me to him.

Do you know what this is? he asks Freddie.

No, Grandad. I don't know.

Well, your mother knows what it is, but she's not saying.

I hated it when he did it then. I hate it now. I hate that he wants me to put words to it. I hate that I'm going to fall for his trick, even with my own son here.

Freddie's looking bewildered, and is embarrassed by the silence.

I wait, watching my father's face watch mine. I make a quick decision.

Quite calmly, I say, *Grandad used to show me that when I was little. He always told me it was sex rearing its ugly head. Isn't that silly?*

* * *

Many people can't recall much of their childhood, but I'm sure my depleted memory store is related to the abuse and its fallout. At times of acute distress, I've searched for the comfort of ordinary homely memories surrounding the beginnings of the loss but I've found blankness.

I have memories of houses. Of rooms in houses. Sometimes I think that if I could find an empty room it might be easier. As it is, I find rooms with dust-sheeted furniture where the forms underneath vanish when I pull away the covers.

I have few clear recollections of my childhood home life, but even fewer memories of school life up to the age of eleven. Some vague, monochrome impressions persist. I think I liked my first school. I think I was proud of my leather satchel and my uniform, a brown-and-white checked dress. I believe I enjoyed going off to the other world of poster paints and Marion Richardson handwriting, but when I push and prod among these impressions, there's nothing of the classrooms I sat in, friends I played with or teachers who taught me.

So I've decided to try another way of rediscovering the past. I'm taking a documentary route. I'm working out how the facts of my school career, gleaned from school reports my mother kept, fit alongside accounts of the same years in her scrapbook of my childhood. Perhaps this will reveal something of what lies under the dust sheets.

Evidently I start at Russell House School in Otford, Kent in May 1960, aged four years and nine months. According to the reports, I'm a pupil there until March 1963. The little girl I read about is foreign to me, but I'm intrigued by these snippets of someone else's life. *Scripture: She remains passive and still sucks her thumb. Poetry: Forming her own taste. Painting: Clear images in well-controlled designs. Arithmetic: Her courage has improved. Geography: A satisfactory beginning to map-making. Writing: Good when she tries.*

The Headmistress, Mrs Nellie Baker, always writes two words at the end of each term's report, alternating between *Very promising* and *Good progress*. At the foot of the report for Easter term 1963, she conflates her stock phrases into *Very good* and adds the send-off, *We wish her success in her new school.* This pile of reports represents the sum total of three years at my first school. It's better than nothing.

Then, in May 1963, after my parents move to Manor Farm, in East Sussex, I begin at Dulwich College Prep School in Cranbrook. I am seven. My two elder brothers are at boarding school. Christopher, at fifteen, has boarded for nine years. David, at nine, has been away for two. My younger brother, Philip, aged two, is at home.

My father, promoted from Mill Manager at Dartford to a management role at Wiggins Teape's Head Office, is commuting by train from Etchingham to Gateway House near St Paul's Cathedral in the City of London. Nanny has moved with us to look after Philip and me. She is living in a cottage near our house and comes to Manor Farm each day. It is she who drives me to and from school. I know this because I can recall her stopping at my favourite sweet shop most afternoons. With a wink and a smile, she treats me to a Mars Bar or a Milky Way to enjoy on the journey.

I shuffle through the pile of reports from DCPS. The first, in June 1963, states, *Clare seems to have settled happily and is doing some very good work.* Looking at the yellowing paper all these decades later, I'm strangely comforted.

This must have been when I began to work, work, work. The *Goods* become *Excellents*. My ranking in the form climbs steadily until by the summer term of 1966 I come top in every subject. I must have left DCPS on quite a high, though I can't remember anything about it.

That same summer term, my report states in the top left corner, *Days absent: 26.* That's more than five weeks, nearly half the term. My mother's scrapbook entries for the period tell of coughs and colds, nothing serious.

I look at all the reports again. From 1963 until 1966 they register *Days absent* at levels between 11 and 26 days each term. I check these absences against my mother's log. There is one serious illness at Easter 1964, suspected meningitis, and I do remember being stretchered into an ambulance and driven from Brightling to Hastings with the lights flashing. I also remember the pain, the fever, the lumbar puncture. I was lucky: after a week in hospital, I made a full recovery. But what of all the other absences? I must have been at home. Was I ill, or exhausted, or just not feeling like going to school? And why doesn't my mother mention these frequent school absences in the scrapbook?

I re-read her entries, more carefully this time. In between the accounts of haircuts and swimming lessons, she describes frequent wild rages, insolence and rudeness as well as contrite notes of apology left on her pillow or pushed under her bedroom door.

Apparently I was forever pleading to be heard. Asking for forgiveness.

The parallel school reports tell of extreme shyness and quietness, sketching a withdrawn but diligent and ordered little girl, who is learning to keep her head down and achieve.

As I sit with the documents spread out in front of me on the table, I begin to understand. Something settles out, like oil and vinegar in a bottle. I'm looking at the records of two girls during the period when my father was abusing me. One, the home-child, is emotionally volatile, swinging between fury and contrition; she adores and needs to be adored by her mother. The other, the school-child, is careful, measured, self-sufficient, almost obsessively tidy; she works harder and harder at her lessons, with better and better results, despite the unexplained school absences.

And then there's a third presence, discernible as a space that both separates and holds together the two girls. This space is like the central image of Rubin's Vase – the black-and-white optical illusion where you can see either a vase or two heads in silhouette, but you can't hold both at once. Logged only in the school reports by *Days absent*, and not evident at all in my mother's scrapbook, this subtle, invisible, hollow child holds the pain and hides the memories. She does the necessary work of forgetting, and she does it thoroughly.

As I dwell on this absent presence, I wonder how and when she came into being. Was she always there, watching from the wings, ready to appear? Did she come alive the first time my father focused the ciné camera on me, or when he looked at me, beckoning? Or perhaps the first time he touched me as a father should never touch his daughter?

However this third part of me – the container child – came

about, I have a sense that she passed between the worlds of home and school like a ghost through a solid door, seeking to console the angry girl or encourage the quiet one to work harder. She must have been responsible for holding the entire act together.

So in this project of trying to reconstruct my early school days, I've found both less and more than I anticipated. And in locating the sometimes invisible container child, I've become aware of a version of me I recognise. I identify with her more than with either of the girls I've read about. She is how I began.

* * *

5 June, 2009
It's June already! This intense late spring is harsh and clear, insistent on life. It seems wrong when I'm having to focus on death and decay. I feel at odds with nature. I want to stop it all and tell it to wait until he's dead, until he's burned and scattered and gone.

It looked as though he might die after last week's long days of sleep. Annabel said, *No, don't worry, he's not dying yet.* But he must be close to the end. I feel the familiar mixture of fear and anticipation.

His swings between denial (up and about, having people to lunch, planning beach trips) and reality (comatose in bed and being woken for medication) come faster and are more extreme, the scales tipping towards the latter as he slides downhill. He'll resist to the very end.

I fantasise about being with him when he dies. The final cut. Meanwhile I plan another visit for Saturday. I think about how to be with him. I find it so difficult, yet I can't *not* see him. The agony of it. The agony in expressing it.

In a little while, on this painful but ecstatic green morning, I will take myself to the white-painted top room, to work. Work will help.

* * *

This time when I visit, he's tearful and tired and not wanting to talk. We're both aware of his avoidance. I feel myself disappear into him because of his need. He sucks me in. The child in me disappears. She is devoured, consumed, and she threatens to pull the adult with her.

I have to be strong. With my strong adult self, I comfort him and give him something like the constant unconditional love of a parent. But he's the parent. He should have done this for me and he never did. His love, such love as he can show, has always been conditional. Do this and I will love you. Be like this and I will love you. Be my mother, sister, wife, daughter – and perfect at each – and I may love you in every way and none. When I see you in this role you become the role. When I'm finished with you in this role, you will revert to another role. This is how it's been.

This morning I want to know who I am as I sit with him at the end. I must try not to resent the relationship he has with others, the shared laughter and jokes as they sit on his bed, the lightness and harmony he enjoys with them when all he gives me is a package of misery to deal with. All my life it's been passed to and fro between us like an endless game of Pass the Parcel.

He thinks I'm my mother and he asks again about my engagement ring. *What's that ring?*

For the umpteenth time I reply, *It's my engagement ring, Dad, bought on our fifth wedding anniversary because we couldn't afford one until then.*

He asks, *Where's the naval crown?* A brooch he gave my mother.

I say, *I have it safely, Dad. Mum gave it to me before she died.*

He drifts into a restful sleep for ten or fifteen minutes while I sit there. When he wakes, he's tearful.

I ask him, *Is there anything you'd like to talk about, Dad?*

He's silent for a few moments, then he says, *No, no.* And he purses his lips and closes his eyes. No. Nothing he will bring out.

I take his hand and squeeze it until I can feel the bones pressing together.

I try to imagine what is on the other side of his dying and his death. I need to know there's *something.* Yes, I'm resilient. Resilience is the other side of shame. I've come through loss and pain, and made many adjustments. I must continue, will continue.

I have to think about all these things. I have to remain in touch with the child me who still wants and misses a father. I have to acknowledge that he has been the father I didn't want, and that he has never been the father I did want. And I have to prepare to lose both.

* * *

THE WORLD ACCORDING TO MY FATHER
12. THE BODY

The human body is like a car.

Providing you keep body and car clean, fuelled and well oiled, and providing of course you have them regularly serviced, they will take you many thousands of miles without breaking down.

When the body breaks down, it should be taken to the doctor who will be able to fix it. A doctor who fails to fix the problems of the human body is not a good doctor. Further medical opinions should be sought as soon as possible.

The human body is entirely separate from the human mind. The mind does not have to be considered or looked after, it just gets on with doing what it does.

The idea of mind and body being in any way linked is absurd, and too complicated and frightening to think about.

* * *

9 June, 2009
I'm agitated this morning at the thought of seeing him again tomorrow. How will I sustain the balance I sometimes manage to find? How will I recreate that calm feeling when I'm physically present with him, sitting in the room with him? How will I hold down my anxieties for the duration of my visit?

Recently, in the middle of the night, I heard someone on the radio say that the opposite of love is fear. That rings true. Those are the two sides of my relationship with him: a weird kind of love and a huge fear, mostly co-existing. A better way of putting it than love and hate.

I think about writing. I wonder how far my writing will help me pick up the bits of fear and love and bind them into one in a way I can't do in my life. Contain the emotions, strap them down and make sense of it all. Like the work I used to do as a bookbinder. Perhaps I will take the sheets of paper, fold them, sew them and make them into a book.

It feels as though my work will never be finished, just as it feels that his life will never be done.

* * *

THE WORLD ACCORDING TO MY FATHER
13. KEYS

Keys are precious and important. They must not be mislaid.

Keys must be carefully labelled and hung on a set of brass hooks near the back door. They should never be left in the lock.

You can't have too many spare sets of keys.

Unlabelled keys are an abomination.

* * *

11 June, 2009

Yesterday, for the first time ever, the back and front doors were locked and I had to ring and knock to gain entry. I was locked out. Or he was locked in.

Once I was inside, I noticed that most of the key hooks by the kitchen door were unoccupied. There were keys placed in locks throughout the house. Some internal doors were locked. Annabel told me later that he had spent several hours doing this.

It was as though he'd been locking up against death. It makes me smile to think of it because I'm sure the Grim Reaper has been in the house for a while already, biding his time. Dad's told me that he hears someone moving about at night. I imagine a dark-cloaked figure creeping from room to room, rearranging the stacks of Uriplan incontinence pads, counting the bottles of Oramorph, padding downstairs to make a cup of instant coffee.

* * *

I arrive at midday when my father's getting up. He's wearing his grey tracksuit, his head poking forward like a crow's. He's hunched and walks slowly.

I sit with him while he eats the toast and strawberry jam Annabel has prepared. His hands are thin, the skin translucent like tissue paper. His skeleton's becoming clearer.

When he's eaten, I settle him in his favourite chair with a rug. I fetch a glass of juice for his dry mouth.

Conversation doesn't really happen. His lip movements are mostly silent. He only occasionally voices something from the continuum in his head. His utterances are like the tips of icebergs. Sometimes I bump into the underwater parts.

You don't seem to be in too much pain, Dad?

None, at the moment. Lots of lip sucking and tongue clicking. Then he speaks again. *Last time you were here, you asked me if there was anything I wanted to tell you. What did you mean?*

You seemed very sad and I thought perhaps you needed to talk.

Well, I wondered what you had in mind?

Dad, it's about what you have in mind.

Oh, I see. He sounds irritable. My reply isn't what he wanted.

He closes his eyes. He bites his lip. His tongue clicks against his upper teeth. After a few seconds his face screws into a tight knot, veins bulging at the temples. His hands grip the arms of the chair. *I'm having a surge. I need Oramorph.*

The dose is already prepared, in a small plastic cup on the table. I lift it to his mouth.

* * *

The truest stories don't have happy endings, nor are they erased or forgotten by years passing. Confession and forgiveness may not follow in the fullness of time. Nothing is clear or obvious.

Some days the scars still itch and pull and I can't forget why I'm this shape. Other days I don't care to remember. Yet other days, a gift arrives, a moment of sheer insight.

Sometimes you don't set out to revisit a place, you simply find you've arrived there. On a hot sunny day in June 2009, I end up in Bexhill-on-Sea by mistake, as though the patterns in my life have conspired to show themselves.

I set out to go to Pevensey but miss the turning. Suddenly I'm driving along that narrow coast road, shingle beach to the right, fields to the left, ending up at Cooden. When I pass the

Cooden Beach Hotel, I'm indicating right onto Richmond Avenue, touching that old stack of memories like a bundle of letters at the bottom of a drawer.

I've thought of this place often, always delighting in the initial lightness of remembering. But whenever I looked closer, I sensed a bottled specimen, beautiful but sealed. I knew that the cries of gulls made me ecstatic, sad, thoughtful all at once but it was as though the feelings themselves were beyond a screen, untouchable.

The understanding has come slowly and with knowing other things. Suddenly this June, here in this place, I understand with my body, and through my body I can reach my emotions. The memory I carry from my grandmother's house in that south-coast seaside town is a potent mix of physical relief, excitement and security. Every sight and sound associated with the place is a positive trigger. This was the place where he hardly ever came. A place of women and children. A safe house. Here, my mother wielded the ciné camera, making short snatches of wobbly film.

I always hoped that one day I'd rediscover the way the gulls' cries lifted my spirits to soar, like them, above the earth. Now I'm here. I listen to the gulls cry and I rise again, just as the small girl used to. I want to laugh and dance.

At last the specimen bottle is broken and I can touch what's inside. Until those contents fade and fall to dust, I'll love them as never before, with a passion that comes of balancing in the stay of memory.

* * *

Ciné film, 1962

Stony beach, wooden breakwater, a thin boy sitting on it, swinging his legs. The shot shifts to a foreground of a tartan rug laid across pebbles. The girl is sitting next to the red-haired boy, who is helping her brush her hair. The camera lingers on the brushing, the boy turning to say something, the girl laughing. Both blow kisses to the camera.

* * *

My grandmother bought her house in Richmond Avenue, on the respectable side of Bexhill-on-Sea, in 1961, shortly before my parents moved to Sussex. She had lived with them since she was widowed in the early 1950s, but this time she didn't move with them. *I want one last home of my own before I get too old*, she told my mother.

She lived there for three years before rheumatoid arthritis stiffened and slowed her and she came back to live with us. But the years of Richmond Avenue might have been thirty or three hundred in my imagination, so powerful was my experience of that house by the sea where Granny ruled and where Granny's things, previously confined to a couple of rooms at our house in Dartford, spilled over and multiplied to fill a four-bedroom house.

Whenever we were there, we divided our days between her house and the beach hut a few minutes' walk away, which she rented for a few pounds a year. I thought of it as *my* house on the pebbles. I used to pack a small blue cardboard attaché case with my favourite dolls and their changes of clothes, and I'd set them up in the beach hut to play while my brothers and I got on with the important business of building sandcastles, chasing waves and collecting stones.

We went to Bexhill at half-term and during the holidays and sometimes for a day at the weekend. We went there with such regularity that I thought of Bexhill as the only alternative to life in my parents' house. There was home, there was Bexhill, and there was the road between the two which we children experienced from the pale-leather back seat of the Rover, blurring our way along nauseous green lanes and through Kentish orchards and villages until at one particular bend after a railway bridge my mother would always ask, *Who can see the sea?*

The Bexhill house rattled with seaside breezes. It was bright with the cries of gulls. My grandmother's garden was planted orange and yellow, pink and red, in crowded flowerbeds. The lawns were kept short and stripy. A low wall boundaried the road so you could watch the top halves of grownups going past.

My grandmother always drew the curtains before dusk, as though she were trying to shut out those moments between light and dark. She said it was a habit from her days in India. In her house, it was either day or night, and once the curtains were drawn it was effectively night. Then, she would pour herself and any adult guest a small dose of ginger wine in a short-stemmed crystal glass. This was the tipple or *chotapeg* before the grownups' evening meal which was served later than our high tea. From my bed, I loved to hear voices in the kitchen below and the clatter of dishes being cleared. To fall asleep at Richmond Avenue was to sink into a sandy oblivion in the sure and certain knowledge of another happy day tomorrow.

In my patchy childhood memory, that house is the place I

loved to be. It bridges my six-year-old self and my eight-year-old self. It has a centrifugal force, a gravity, pulling both of me into the centre and linking us in its bracing saline energy.

This is the only house of my childhood that I'd like to return to. I'd run my hands over its fabric and find the seams where the awareness of the first child meets that of the second. I'd be glad to reacquaint myself with the gas grill, the scent of ginger wine, the obliging heads of snapdragons.

* * *

Ciné film, 1963
Richmond Avenue. A series of slow shots around an Edwardian-style garden laid out with wide herbaceous borders and straight-edged paths. A mass of colour: chrysanthemums, snapdragons, dahlias. Occasional glimpses through to other houses, other gardens. A road. Cars passing beyond a pale-green garden gate. The camera comes to rest on four children leaning against a red-brick wall by the kitchen door, licking ice lollies. The shot wobbles. Cut to a pebbly beach. In the foreground the girl puts stones into a bucket, one at a time.

* * *

15 June, 2009
I've been thinking how extraordinary it is that he should remember, despite all the drugs and the comatose periods, our conversation of a week ago.

Last time you were here, you asked me if there was anything I wanted to tell you. What did you mean?

You seemed very sad and I thought perhaps you needed to talk.
Well, I wondered what you had in mind?
Dad, it's about what you have in mind.

Thinking about the exchange helps to soothe me. Something has been voiced, though not properly spoken and not heard by him.

It seems he won't speak and he can't hear me. He tells me all the time that he can't hear me. Can't bear to hear me, perhaps.

I come and go from the death chamber. When I go into his space, I rely on my own way of being with him, listening and sitting with the feelings in the place of silence, his place of not speaking and not hearing.

I can't and won't force him to talk. I want to feel him struggle with it. To demand and confront would allow him the opportunity to deny it. I'm not going to give him that chance.

* * *

THE WORLD ACCORDING TO MY FATHER
14. TRUTH

Truth has many guises.

Truth is a fine idea but it cannot be spoken.

Many true things are likely also to be painful so it is best to put them away and keep them out of sight.

However, sometimes the truth tends to leak out. The gaps where it might filter through must be stopped-up carefully.

Truth can become distorted by thought, another reason not to delve into the human mind or examine it closely.

The truth is often dull. If truth is embellished and made into a story, this can be told over and over again until it becomes the new truth. Then the original truth can be forgotten.

Truth is an unruly child. It must be watched because it is seldom obedient.

* * *

While the cliff hideaway might have been a secure place for my father, neither the place itself nor the idea of it was secure for me. Nowhere felt safe with him.

I don't actually think anything bad happened there. It probably was a safe place. But I never really knew the difference – how could I?

Anyway, I'm making my memory of the cliff as whole and true as I can. I'm working at remaking it. I've polished it now until it gleams.

We return to the holiday house from the morning surf, rinse off the salt and sand, change into jeans and T-shirts and woollen jumpers.

He says, *Shall we go to our favourite place?*

And I say, *Yes, Daddy.*

We leave the garden through the blue gate in the corner and traverse the gently shelving turf, turning right onto the cliff path.

To find the approach to our secret place, we have to negotiate a fence. Then there is a narrow track through bracken and gorse as tall as me. Here my father swings me up to sit astride his shoulders.

The sea spreads out before us like a great sheet of beaten pewter, and there is the cliff edge, or at least the first edge, the one we will have to drop below to get to our hidden ledge.

My father sings, *He who would valiant be 'gainst all disaster, let him in constancy follow the Master.* His steps are slower and more careful as we approach the edge, then he slips me over his right shoulder and sets me to the ground a few feet short of the drop.

I'll go first, he says.

He sits on the right angle of granite and launches himself over, pushing off with his arms. His body and head disappear over the edge and for a minute I'm alone on the clifftop, at the crest of the world. I hear his voice again, from below, distant and muffled by the wind.

Okay, come slowly to the edge. Squat first, and sit down.

I do exactly as he says, and in a moment I'm in his arms, half flying and half falling onto the ledge, which is only as wide as my parents' bed, and a little longer.

We sit with our backs to the cliff wall and our feet pointing out to sea, the music of the waves booming up to us. We are hostages to raucous herring gulls and the rush of clouds. Nobody knows we're here. Nobody can see us.

* * *

Ciné film, 1964
Manor Farm. The girl is wearing blue shorts and a white polo shirt. Her hair is short. She stands on flagstones, in front of a low garden wall. Four dolls are arranged carefully on a wooden chair

beside her. The camera zooms in on the girl's face. She says
something, squinting into the sun, and gestures towards the dolls
on the chair.

* * *

Where I live now, I have a garden. The earth is pale and poor where chalk mingles with precious topsoil, a thin dry layer of white and grey.

I was excited the day I dug my vegetable patch from rough grass, knowing no one had touched the ground in years. I found a china doll's head, broken off at the neck, soil filling the space inside. I washed out her head and put it on the bathroom windowsill, wondering where her body was. And kept on digging.

The ground is full of flint and lumps of chalk rising, rising as I dig. I've dug for ten years and still the chalk and flint float upwards. Spring after spring, I heap the risen stones.

* * *

Transcript:
We decided to move from Dartford and I — well, what I felt in those days was where on earth could I find a house that I could afford for four children? And the answer of course was you had to go out further and East Sussex was good for children. So we bought Manor Farm. Actually Granny bought it, in 1962. A big house and it had a flat for her. Fifteen acres of grounds — wonderful gardens with rhododendrons and azaleas

138

and an enormous swimming pond. She bought all
of that for twelve thousand pounds in 1962 and
we lived there for twelve years pretty much,
and I commuted to London.[Laughing…] I remember
when we first moved in there we kept finding fine
bottles of whisky all-round the house in funny
little corners. The woman who lived there before
was an alcoholic.

* * *

That house – Manor Farm. The first time I heard the name I
thought there must be cows and sheep and tractors but it had
not been a farm in over a hundred years and the original
farmhouse had long ago burned down. Our house was built in
the 1930s.

I've been back there many times and I've never been back, I've
dreamed it and nightmared it. I'm part of it and it's part of me.

The ground froze so deep the winter of 1962, just after my
parents bought the place, that the builders couldn't dig the
foundations for the extension to the kitchen. The steep drive was
iced up for two or three months so they couldn't get their lorries
up and down, or that's how the story went.

I don't remember that. I remember going to the house for the
first time in late March 1963, the sun out and the daffodils
blowing in wild seas, and patches of grainy snow still lying in
shaded corners. I'd never seen such a big garden, such an
enormous house.

There was no furniture inside. I assumed that was how we were
going to live, without tables, chairs, beds or curtains. I liked the

idea. It was airy and free, an adventure after the ordered life with Granny at Richmond Avenue where I'd been staying with Nanny while my parents moved.

This is just a picture, my first impression: bright cool sky and wide sloping lawns with smears of yellow in long grass. A picnic lunch indoors, my mother excited about her new kitchen and her dream garden. I want to go upstairs, want to know which bedroom I'll have, where my brothers will sleep. I want to see the view from each window. I'm impatient to be living here.

I feel that impatience now. These days I can slip myself back into that seven-year-old skin as though I'm putting on an old coat. I am both child and adult trying to remember.

The child remembering this is like the doll in my vegetable patch – her head and body parted company and were strangers for a long time. Her head filled with earth. Now the parts might be able to join up again.

At Manor Farm, there are lots of different rooms on different floors. Long passages, corners and cupboards, attics. Outside – trees, bushes, long grass. Summer houses, sheds. Lots of places to hide or stay hidden when your mother's calling and doesn't know where you are. Places to be led to or followed from. Quiet places to keep secrets. A world as big as a small village with just a few of us living there. An idyll. How privileged we are, how lucky, all that freedom. No questions asked.

From age seven to eighteen I'm there, trapped in that place, in all its beauty and space.

* * *

The letter was written on blue paper and sent in a matching blue envelope. Basildon Bond, I should think.

The envelope, which had been opened roughly along the top, was addressed to an eight-year-old me. It was written by Margaret Baker, the woman who was our nanny when my brothers and I were growing up at Manor Farm in the 1960s.

It must be fifteen years since I saw the letter and I can't remember exactly what it said. Nanny always wrote when she was away on holiday. I expect she enquired how I was getting on at school and she might have told me about the weather in Scotland, or how she had been to the pictures in Aberdeen with her brother, Ted. She sent lots of love. It was not a long letter. The handwriting, as I recall, covered just the front and half the back, of one small sheet of paper.

It's a mystery how the envelope containing the letter ended up behind the full-length wall mirror in my parents' bedroom in that house near Brightling. Perhaps my eight-year-old self had put it there for safekeeping.

The letter was behind the mirror for thirty-two years.

It was there while my parents turned in their sleep each night, it was there as the sun came up over the silver birch trees, there the day we set off for London in 1965 to see Winston Churchill's funeral procession; in July 1969 when we all crowded on to the big bed to watch my father's new television showing men walking on the moon.

It was there in 1972 when I left school, in 1973 when the packers arrived to dismantle the big bed and my mother's dressing table and heave them into a pantechnicon destined for the new house in Wiltshire. It was there as the Brightling house stood cold and echoey for weeks before the next family moved in.

The letter stayed behind the mirror, undisturbed, through the 70s, the 80s, the early-90s, while serial sets of owners occupied the house, while swathes of narcissi turned the paddocks gold and then brown. It was there all through Thatcher's long reign. It was there as Tony Blair was elected leader of the Labour Party in 1994. It was there on the day when, many miles away, I met the man I would marry, and still there when I gave birth to our son in 1995.

In 1996, the house changed hands again. The new people decided to strip out and refurbish the main bedroom. When they unscrewed the long mirror from the wall, the letter fell to the floor. They recognised the name on the envelope because a few weeks earlier, when they had shown their friend Elizabeth some pictures of the house they were buying, she said she knew a family who had lived there years and years ago. She had even visited them once or twice in the 1960s.

So the new owners sent the blue letter to Elizabeth in case she wanted to pass it on to the family she knew who had lived there. She and my mother had stayed in touch since they were at school together, though by 1996 my mother was ill with dementia. But Elizabeth had my father's address so she sent him the letter from behind the mirror and he forwarded it to me, along with her covering note.

I wrote back to her straightaway, intrigued by the uncanny circle and delighted to make contact with my mother's oldest friend. We had plenty to talk about. And it turned out that my mother had asked Elizabeth to be godmother to the infant me, a role she had reluctantly turned down because she did not share my parents' religious beliefs.

Elizabeth introduced me to the people who had found Nanny's

blue letter. They, in turn, invited me to revisit the Brightling home of my childhood and I went there a few times over the following years. They were kind and hospitable and I was glad to go back, more or less ready to meet the memories and the ghosts.

I don't know where the letter is now. When I thought about it, I looked everywhere but it's lost again.

* * *

18 June, 2009
A long day out to see Dad yesterday.

He's between here and the next world. He sways and swings and I swing too. Between wanting to see him and not, between feeling sad and feeling calm, between agony and relief.

He seems to be letting go of life, hardly eating now except a few spoonfuls of Heinz Cream of Chicken Soup or part of a light omelette, swallowed with water and an anti-nausea tablet. Anything more and he brings it straight back up. His hands are bony and bruised, his eyes and cheeks hollowing. His entire body is in retreat, no longer resisting the cancer.

It's easier to be in his space now, with the rule book lying dusty in the corner. You can sit where you want to, leave your things around, cross and re-cross the boundaries between different parts of the house. Yesterday, I took that sign off his kitchen door – the one that said *Kids Keep Out* – and threw it in the bin.

Much of the time he's asleep. Sixteen or eighteen hours at a stretch. Each time he wakes he's somewhere different. Yesterday, when his eyes opened, he was in Scotland. He thanked me for moving him to Scotland, for rearranging everything so neatly and for staying with him.

A wonderful gathering, he said. *And the heather in bloom. It's unusually warm for Scotland.*

Perhaps he'd heard his grandchildren's voices from the garden as they played quick cricket and it took him back to his time at Stoneywood in Aberdeenshire. He and my mother lived there for a year from April 1947 when they were newly married and he was a trainee papermaker. Perhaps something about daytime sleeping reminds him of working night shifts and napping during the day.

I haven't seen your mother for a long time, he said. *Do you know where she is?*

Feeling a coward I said, *She's around somewhere, Dad.*

Is she asleep? he asked.

Yes. A long sleep.

It's all true. It's more than ten years since she died.

I wonder what films are playing in his head. I wonder if he's making the final edits.

* * *

Transcript:

I was up in Scotland learning about papermaking.
Then we were married in 1947. And I must tell
you about how I got married. [Laughing…] It was
the custom at Stoneywood if somebody was getting
married, that the girls in the salle (of which
there were a couple of hundred), they got hold
of you and took your trousers off and laid you

144

out on the bench and blacked you all over with carbon black which is dreadful stuff. Apart from smelling, it's terribly difficult to get rid of. And I was in a hell of a mess. I did my best with towels and I couldn't get the bloody stuff off. And I got on the sleeper train to go down to London for my wedding. And this chap Giles was on the train too and he knew I was getting married and he knew what the problem was and he said, Well there's only one thing we can do and that is buy a couple of bottles of whisky. (Which you could do in those days from the chap who kept the sleepers). It was remarkable because whisky was in very short supply but you could always get it on the sleepers.[Laughing...] So we bought a couple of bottles and I lay down in the sleeper and Giles got a cloth and the whisky and he got most of this carbon black off. And of course in between rubbing this off and general hoo-ha we had the best part of a bottle of whisky between us and I arrived in London the next morning in rather poor shape.

* * *

My mother used to wake me in the mornings when I was a child. I was aware of the sound of the bedroom door opening over the carpet, her tentative step into the room, sometimes even her breathing as she stood by the bed. She would stand very still, as if getting ready to appear, then she would walk through the grey-and-pink shadows to the window, draw the curtains and be there. A vision in the early light. Next she produced her soft warm voice like a rabbit from a hat. I loved the way she delivered me into the day.

My mother, who was so skilled at appearing, never fully mastered the art of disappearing, although it was something she studied for a number of years later in her life. She used to retire to her bedroom for a rest in the afternoon, often taking with her the newspaper and a box of chocolates. These were her props. These trial disappearances were, however, short-lived and too often seemed inadequate to her purpose. When she reappeared after an hour or so, she looked tired, as though she'd been trying too hard.

My father's more regular presence, following his retirement in 1984, further diminished her ability to disappear. It was as though the emphasis of him in the house closed off her routes to disappearance. Around him she felt the compulsion to manifest herself physically and emotionally, and he insisted she be there. That was when she began to retreat inside herself – the real disappearance.

No longer permitted to sometimes literally disappear, she found what refuge she could in the hidden places of her mind. Her dementia grew slowly but steadily: it was to rub her out almost completely in her last years.

My father knows everything there is to know about disappearing. His own mother vanished permanently when he was five, causing his father to disappear for long periods. His brother John disappeared forever, sunk in a submarine, when my father was sixteen. Since then, over a period of nearly seventy years, he has practised coming and going from his country, from his family. And, of course, from himself.

His disappearances have been so many, so varied and at times so dramatic that it would be impossible to catalogue them. They take many forms. He can disappear at close or long range, in person or on the phone, quickly or slowly, physically or mentally, or with a combination of techniques that leaves you astonished and impressed.

The best of his appearances are rare and precious, standing out vividly in memory, often because of the disappearance that precedes or follows them. And because he's so unpredictable, a good appearance can be a comfort, something you straightaway put in a special place to keep safe because you're not sure if there'll be another.

* * *

Many years have passed since my father asked me to take my mother away from him and from her own home, to a care home. He could no longer cope with her dementia. He disappeared that day and left me to it.

There are times when love is impossibly difficult; I was taking her away to a place where the care would be better than my father's, but to remove her from her home was to strip away the layers of sacred meaning she had given herself. She was seventy-two.

If there was a film, it would run like this.

The opening frames show my mother waking in the night. She turns onto her right side and extends her arm to press the repeater on a chiming carriage clock which strikes four. She closes her eyes, lies back for a few seconds on the pillow, reaches out again to press the repeater. Her lips move as she counts.

I wake in our flat in West London at six, tiptoe along the passage to check on Freddie, who's curled asleep in his cot. I make a mug of tea and take it back to bed. I think of my father's call yesterday, how he'd said to me, *I can't go on for even one more day*. How I'd immediately phoned the care home I'd decided on, and asked if they could take my mother.

By now, she is walking in her garden, wearing a dressing gown loosely wrapped around her and unmatched shoes. Her route is haphazard – she zigzags across the lawn from one border to another, looks up at the breezy September sky, squats to study daisies in the grass.

It might be a split screen now. As she deadheads a climbing rose on the left screen, on the right I mix Freddie's breakfast milk, pack a bag for him and one for me. Half an hour later we're on our way. He's asleep again in his car seat in the back as we queue in traffic on the A3.

I stop on the way and leave nine-month-old Freddie with my mother-in-law Ruth who, at eighty-one, is still immensely active and capable. She and Duncan reared six children of their own and are both doctors so I'm leaving Freddie in the best of hands. He is calm and effusive with them, and he's stayed with them several times before. Tonight he'll sleep there in a travel cot.

I think to myself, *Perhaps I don't have to make the last part of the journey. Instead we can stay with Ruth and Duncan for an hour or two and then drive back to London.*

But in reality, what happens is that I leave Freddie and his overnight bag, and after a few private minutes with Ruth, I drive the last two miles to my parents' house, park at the back and sit in the car for a minute or two to compose myself.

In the kitchen, the dogs get up from their beds to greet me. My father's breakfast dishes are stacked on the counter, but there's no sign of him or my mother. Sunlight falls in a band from the east-facing window across the formica worktops. I notice the window is cobwebbed. Since my last visit, two weeks ago, an African violet on the sill has died of neglect. Its leaves are crisp and brown. The soil has shrunk to a hard ball in the pot.

A home of twenty years is a lifetime of memories. She made the memories as she made the home. Now she's losing both.

They moved to Monks House in the drought summer of 1976, the grass yellow already, and sand from the garden gusting through the house. By the following spring, it was all green again. She enjoyed the Jersey cows in the field at the bottom of the garden; when they came towards her, she spoke to them. She enjoyed the giant beech tree on the lawn – she used to cut tightly-budded branches from it every spring and bring them into the house to watch the leaves open. We buried three of her beloved dogs at the foot of that tree. She grew English roses against the south-facing brick of the house, and she cursed and marvelled at the deer who grazed on their flower buds.

There are too many things about this place she has loved and the risks of these loves are manifold. As she has demented, she has stayed here more and more, growing tense and fearful at the suggestion of travel or even short visits elsewhere. She long since became a hostage to the place and to her affection for it. Her home, her refuge, is finally her prison.

And now I've been summoned here to take her from it.

On the top sheet of a pad of paper, my father has made a list of what needs to go with her and he's left it on the kitchen table knowing I'll see it: *Pills, Night things, Sponge bag, Slippers, Hairbrush, Mirror.* There are notes too, in another list on another sheet of paper. A kind of justification: *She can no longer brush her own teeth. She is not happy here. She cries at night. I am exhausted. I can't get out to see friends.*

By the time he emerges from his study, I've had plenty of time to read his lists. He planned it like that.

How was your journey?

I made good time. The traffic was light.

She's upstairs. She's all dressed and ready. I've put a bag out for you to pack her things into.

He pauses, flicks the kettle switch on. *Look, I'm not sure she'll go there with me, I think she'll go more easily with you...* His voice peters out. I'll be doing this on my own.

I go upstairs, guessing where I'll find her. She's sitting on their bed. She doesn't look up. I sit down next to her, take her hands in mine, cradle them, feeling the smooth almond-shaped fingernails, the enlarged thumb joints. We stay like this for some minutes before I stroke her cheek and kiss her forehead.

I've no idea what to do next.

Beyond the bedroom window, a light wind is bending the pair of birch trees in the south-west corner of the garden. A few leaves are caught and snatched on the moving air. September, a month of change; this year it seems unbearable. I want to erase everything that has culminated in being here today. I want never to have known my mother's creeping illness, my father's demands, the careful intricate planning that has brought me to this point – phone calls to doctors and nursing homes, visits to locked and unlocked institutions, despairing at the multiple flaws of each.

This morning she doesn't seem too unlike her old self. Is it because she has sensed what today is about and has summoned all her courage to accept it? Or is it one of those miracle days that arrives like a gift from the past? This has happened before. My father has phoned to say things are really bad and I've rushed from London only to find her laughing and smiling, hospitable, remembering who I am. And my heart fractures, again.

When we come to it, the next stage of the departure is remarkably plain and straightforward. Before I have a chance to try and tell her that I'm taking her to a care home, my mother announces she'd like to show me around her house. It's as though she knows she's moving and sees me as a potential tenant. She takes me on a tour, room by room, showing me the view from each window, telling me fragments of stories about paintings and furniture as we go.

I've always loved this place, she says, as we stand by the French windows in the wide hallway at the bottom of the stairs. We stood here on my wedding day, before the photographer came, before she was so ill. Now we gaze out together across her garden and I know she knows she's leaving and won't come back.

Half an hour later, she climbs into the passenger seat of my car as I load her suitcase into the boot. When I go to shut the dogs in, I notice she's left her handbag behind on the kitchen table.

* * *

Ciné film, 1959

A wide bay. Sand, pale-blue sky flecked with dust motes. The girl, wearing a blue swimsuit, pulls an inflatable duck behind her as she wades through a rock pool. She's freckled and her hair is bleached. Two boys are digging to her left. She walks over to watch them. The camera follows. In the background, base camp – a blue-and-orange beach tent. Adult women in shorts and jumpers sit on folding chairs next to a small portable cooker. Cut to a small boy in tartan trousers and blue sweater, sitting on a picnic rug. The woman presents him with a cake with six lit candles. He is handed a knife and shown how to cut the cake, which he does with great deliberation. Cut to brown bear pacing up and down in a cage, with its cub. Camera wobble. Close-up shot of a lioness behind bars.

* * *

20 June, 2009

Rain, heavy rain, my white roses dumped on the ground and the windows steamed up.

Dad's very sick and has become doubly incontinent. Called his doctor today. Discussed whether these symptoms might be caused by antibiotics, and if so should we stop giving them. Then into another Living Will discussion. Dad's quality of life is sometimes reasonable but the periods of reasonable are shorter and shorter and the periods of degradation – falls and wounds and infections – are becoming more frequent, longer and more severe.

Meanwhile he's still travelling. Brazil, Australia, Belgium, frequently Scotland. There are fewer times when he's properly lucid. He leads a split life between reality and escape. These two strands of his existence, the knowing and the not knowing, have always been there but have become more extreme.

* * *

I learned it from my parents. I too can appear and disappear.

Now it is I, not my mother, who makes an appearance every morning. I wake myself up, watch myself creep to the bathroom. I sit on the bed and wait for myself to dress. I keep an eye, making sure I do the things I need to do in the way I should do them.

When I disappear, I do it privately, for short periods. I tend to come back as soon as I can.

* * *

I first visited Florence in March 1970, with my mother. I came again in spring 1973, in my gap year, in love with the place. I stayed eight weeks, taking courses in Italian and history of art. In November 1983, down to my last hundred pounds after a few months studying and travelling as a bookbinder, I roomed for a while in a *pensione* near the Duomo where the signora cooked over an open fire. In 1993, I came here with Philip, the year after we married. Now, in June 2009, I am back with Freddie for a week. It's such a treat.

In Florence, I am happy to be incapable of anything but sensory existence, the here and now, retracing old ways around the city as though in search of my old selves. Collecting up the pieces.

I stand on the Ponte Vecchio as the city sets about going to work. Looking across to Lungarno Guicciardini, where at the age of fifteen I woke and stared at a muddy swell of Arno, I remember being amazed at the past and the future running together and the water flowing so fast. Now it seems slow, but eddying in swirls.

There are so many layers in this city. Layers of history and invention, layers of stories. Layers of me I can't even touch but from which I draw comfort, sensing them like echoes of voices in a church when you linger after the congregation has left.

I'm adding another layer this time, with Freddie. Creating his memories from moments of mine, of ours, revisiting places I remember my mother first showing me. We even take parallel photographs, he with his particular way of looking, and I with mine. He's placing me here, in his memory. I hope he'll come back, perhaps in thirty or forty years and lay down his present and let it touch the past for a while.

There are reassuring constants. The scent of fried onions at ten in the morning as thousands of people around the city prepare their next meal. The way the grey women in their pinafore aprons lean out of upper windows and assess the sky before deciding which way to adjust the shutters. Washing strung across balconies and flat roofs. Cranes swinging above the monuments and churches, rebuilding the old stones. Swifts diving and wheeling over the tiles, their cries high-pitched.

Being here might make me sad but it doesn't. The solidity of stone, and the fantasy of no time passing make this place a gift when life is rushing by, when past and present keep colliding in the painful way they have been for the past few years.

I enjoy the paradox of stopping here or there where I may or may not have stopped before – this street corner, that café, a cool church, a familiar bend in the river – and the pleasure of knowing nothing has changed and everything has changed. The sensation of walking by and touching feelings and events long gone, being led by my imagination to the next sensation.

This is a city of curious constancy, a city that spins its people out into the world and at the same time draws visitors into its own clock machinery, where every day is for inventing a mason's pulley, a new pigment, a novel flavour of *gelato*. A city where every moment has been before and has never happened. Where memory is written in stone or not at all.

* * *

30 June, 2009
Ten days since I wrote here. Time away in Italy not thinking of Dad very much, time for me and Freddie, and time for my now and then selves.

I sent Dad a letter before we went to Florence and a card that Freddie signed too. I worried he never had it, never read it, wondered to myself why I hadn't kept a copy. I even imagined he'd torn it up. But when I explained to Annabel how important it was, she searched for it and found it. Then Dad read it several times. Once I knew this, I breathed again. My words had on some level been received. The letter expressed how I cared for him. It matters to me that he read it although I don't understand why.

Yesterday when I went to visit, he ate lunch sitting in bed, having returned from a painful catheter change at hospital. He seemed glad to see me.

My eye fell on the volume of Robert Frost by his bed, the one I gave him for Christmas. I picked it up and examined it for evidence of use. I don't think he's ever opened it.

* * *

THE WORLD ACCORDING TO MY FATHER
15. READING

Reading for pleasure in the daytime is to be thoroughly discouraged. A healthy outdoor activity is much better for a person than lounging around with a book.

People who spend a lot of time reading books should arouse suspicion. Why are they not doing something more useful outdoors?

There is nothing better than a fine adventure story which may be read at night before turning out the light.

Reading for work can be a chore but it is more authentic than reading for pleasure.

A newspaper should be read throughout so as not to waste it. If there isn't time to read it all in one sitting, articles may be cut out and kept for another occasion and the part of the newspaper already read may then be disposed of so as not to litter the house with old papers.

A person who is reading a newspaper should on no account be spoken to or otherwise interrupted.

* * *

Books have always been my comfort and my challenge, my undercover life and my outer clothing. They also remain some of my own dearest secrets. I love to be with books but I don't like to talk about them much. The meanings of poems and stories and the significance of the words in them – these things fit, one inside the next inside the next. Books are Russian dolls, holding delight within delight, brightly-coloured and mysterious. They contain elements that can't and shouldn't be prised out of them. If the book is to retain its integrity, its different layers can no more be separated than the layers of the Earth's crust.

I like to observe how the writing in a book works, and then let it be. I'll ponder books, but I'm reluctant to dissect them. That feels like a violation and can lead to other more serious violations. The very idea of a book club is anathema to me – a number of people all reading the same book and then discussing it. For me, reading is an intensely intimate activity. I go alone to the secret world of a book to observe the repeated reinvention of language.

On my sixth birthday, my mother gave me *The Golden Treasury of Poetry*, selected and with a commentary by Louis Untermeyer, illustrated by Joan Walsh Anglund.

I was still in my nightdress, sitting on the floor by my parents' bed early that summer morning when my mother handed me the parcel. Its weight was shocking and marvellous because I knew it was a book. Secret of secrets: a book wrapped up and disguised, yet known to be one of its kind!

In the pages of that book I first found Blake's *Songs of Innocence* and poems by Robert Frost, Emily Dickinson, Lewis Carroll, Keats, Shelley, Browning, Kipling, Walter de la Mare, Edward Lear, Gerard Manley Hopkins and Ogden Nash. My real life had begun.

Now I can hardly bear to handle, let alone to look at this book because the physical memories are so powerful and the emotions evoked so true and undiluted. The commentator's links and introductions, with their clues to context and their hints at the vast universe of poetry lying beyond this volume, made an impact as great as the poems themselves. When I take the book off the shelf, I feel that it contains all the layers of meaning that books and reading hold for me. This one book is a metaphor for my feelings about books, about words. It is whole and complete and private, possessing those secrets it always possessed and yet more because I've loved it and invested it with my emotions. I have told this book my secrets, even as it told me its own.

* * *

14 July, 2009

The eve of my birthday. I've never much liked the month of July. Dark greens, humidity, the year already over the top. I would prefer to have been born in June or on a brisk late September morning, or perhaps in early spring.

Annabel had to call 999 twice last night whilst Dad raved in psychological pain that seems to be indistinguishable from physical pain. He's the child again, crying and screaming for attention.

As he cracks open, I am more and more secure in my own identity. I'm no longer wholly entangled with him. I'm getting clearer and clearer.

Everything is unspooling.

A new, deep wound on his leg, from a bad fall, has healed despite the doctor's predictions.

He has been having visitors all week. The mood swings continue between bullish, bullying, expansive and quiet, sad, sleepy. He swings more wildly all the time. Annabel confided in me yesterday that his mental state isn't like anything she has ever witnessed in her many years of caring, and definitely neither dementia nor drug-induced. She describes it as *part of his personality*.

He insists on discussing sex with her.

11 August, 2009

The day after my last entry, flowers came with a card, at four o'clock on the afternoon of my birthday. The doorbell rang, and there was a huge bouquet standing on my doorstep. So beautiful. I took the flowers in, sat down and cried. It was as though they had been in the fridge all those years since my birth.

My house was full of his gift, the scent of lilies and pinks. The scent of sorry, maybe, or the scent of regret? That's what I want to think.

I know Annabel arranged it all, but it's still wonderful.

The time of returning. School, swifts flying southwards, new starts, back to work, leaves falling. The sun's lower and the days are shorter but often warm. One of my favourite times of year.

We're just back from Lago Maggiore. I'm remembering a year ago, the storm the night before we left, how I felt about coming back to Dad's dying. Again I come back to that.

* * *

In the recurring dream, I'm sitting in the front passenger seat of an old car – it could be a Morris 1100. A woman is driving. Is it a friend, a relative, my mother, an older me? Everything feels safe with this woman.

The car is travelling along a country road, an empty road, in England. All green fields and hedgerows with thorn blossom, white and palest pink. Idyllic spring weather, clichés for clouds.

We talk a bit, from time to time, eyes fixed on the road ahead. The woman's voice is all around and somehow I know she can hear me clearly. The conversation goes on a long time. Then suddenly she pulls the wheel over to the left. The car rocks down into a ditch, up out of the ditch again. Through a hedge. I hear thorns scratching against glass, an unbearably painful sound. I'm tumbled in my seat, jerked from side to side. I'm convinced I'm about to die. The woman is gripping the wheel and the car is still moving. She says, *It's okay, don't worry*. But the vehicle is out of control.

Next, the car is travelling across a stubble field. This begins to feel exciting. The pleasure of it goes on for many minutes.

Then we lurch and bang to a stop.

The woman calmly turns the key in the ignition and the engine quiets. She stays for a moment in the driver's seat, silent. Then she tells me to get out, quickly, and remove the contents of the car boot. Together we haul out old boxes, trunks and suitcases, piles of clothes, books, full bin bags.

* * *

22 September, 2009

I've had some good talks with Annabel recently. There's so much mutual respect and affection now. And we know we need each other so we can do what we have to do for my father. *We're both angels*, she tells me on the phone.

Dad groped her the other day, amidst a lot more talk of sex. Apparently he said, *Here, give us a suck of those tits.*

When I go to see him, it's very difficult. I feel so stirred up. I'm not sure how to be his kind daughter any more. I'm dealing with too many of my own emotions.

I have to follow my intuition and limit the number of visits I make. Once a fortnight is enough, and then not for long. I have to continue learning how to disentangle myself from him.

I went to see him on Friday. He told me, *What horrid boots, and with those black trousers. I wouldn't like those boots up my backside. But I love my daughter...*

* * *

161

25 September, 2009

Dental check-up yesterday after work. All kinds of other errands too. It's a relief to be out of the house, even to sit on a train and read.

* * *

The dentist says, *Now*. That's the signal he's ready to begin. *Now*. The 'this is it' of words.

In your way, you're ready too, as you have learned to be. You know to open your mouth obediently. Open as wide as you can because otherwise he will say, *Open wider*. And you prefer not to be told again. So you close your eyes.

You're in the dark, tense red dark. You open your mouth; wider, wider, like the snake that disconnects its lower and upper jaws to ingest large prey. Only he isn't your prey. You're his.

There's a jump in your chest that radiates outwards until it reaches hands and fingers, knees and toes, even the top of your head. Moisture comes out of your palms and from under your arms. Around your groin. You're rigid all over by the time he begins to probe your mouth.

You think you can feel his breath on your neck and in your hair and on different parts of your face.

Sometimes he leans over you, looks down through your skull and into your head, reading your thoughts. Mostly you're aware of his hands. How large they are around your face, how the dark red behind your eyes becomes darker or lighter depending on where his hands are. Then there's his voice. His commands. His commentary. *Move your head to the right a little, towards me. Yes, that's good. You can swallow. A bit of pressure now. Not much longer.*

Your jaw's beginning to ache at the hinges just below your ears. You close it a little, then open it just a bit farther than before. Keep it moving. Saliva builds up along your gums and under your tongue.

As he removes the instruments briefly or swaps them for others, you manage a quick gagging half-swallow, a small taken-for-granted miracle of co-ordination.

When at last he's finished, you open your eyes, close your mouth and sit up. You rinse and rinse with mouthwash, ten or twelve times, asking for the glass to be refilled.

* * *

Ciné film, 1960
Cornwall. The ciné camera pans too quickly across impossibly golden hills, a charcoal sky. The shot pulls in to foreground the man and the girl at opposite sides of a large sandcastle. The man's trousers are rolled up to just below the knee. The girl is wearing red shorts and a dark blue sweater. They're both digging, heaping sand onto the pyramid between them. The girl, being unable to reach high enough to raise the summit, adds sand to the sides. Much of it simply falls away. But she takes care to smooth the side of the sandcastle after each spadeful. Meanwhile the man flattens the top, coming down hard with the back of his spade, then increasing the height with more and more sand. Neither man nor girl seems aware of the camera on them.

* * *

26 September, 2009

Much cooler at night. I'm sleeping better because of that.

Spiders spinning at every doorway and across every windowpane.

Late dragonflies in the garden.

* * *

The Missing List

Parts of me are lost and beyond reach. I'll always be without them. I have a constant feeling of loss and hollowness. Even now, after all these years. The pain goes on ambushing me at odd times.

Good memories of my father – I don't seem to have any.

Entire tracts of my memory. They are scattered to the four winds.

My childhood. My adolescence. Where are they? I'd like them back now that I understand they're gone but I know this can't happen.

A sense of where I came from. That is strangely absent. I've had to build the notion of who I am.

My mother. She's missing and I miss her. I want to talk to her, I want to ask her what she knew and didn't know.

Knowing. I'm not sure if it would be better or worse to know more. I live in a state of unknowing.

Self-esteem. Although I've learned about it, it is still missing.

Hundreds or thousands of nights of sleep, all gone.

My brothers. How I miss them. The family is broken. My father broke it.

Special events, parties, big occasions. I missed so many because I was too anxious or too ill to attend.

Joy – this was stolen from me.

Trust. I have problems with trust. Sometimes I trust too much, sometimes I can't trust at all.

Once my father's gone, I think I'll forever be relieved he's dead. I doubt he'll be on the list of what I miss, of what's missing. But I'll miss not being able to miss him.

How can I say what else is on this list when all I know is that so many things are missing?

* * *

The view from my window, in the attic room where I write, tells of autumn. There's still green in the leaves, though not in all of them, and some warmth in the sun at its highest.

The wind is from the east – dry, quirky and gusty, bringing a warning of winter from the cool centre of Europe, bending the great oaks and the lone cedar against their normal flex, scattering litter in the road. The light is watery and clear. Smoke drifts over the town in brownish grey plumes from a garden bonfire. And on every side, the chalk Downs rise above it all, cloud shadows crossing and re-crossing their snooker-table slopes.

This day is shorter than the last and tomorrow will be shorter again, a three-month downhill ride to the end of December.

Here's where my year begins. I like to start new cycles of work and thought as the grass cuttings rot down and the leaves let go. As things settle. I see leaf buds fatten, field mice come out for berries and birds feed to build up their weight for winter, and I know that without this long slow run towards the end, there can be no spring, no growth the other side of winter.

What does it mean to survive? I don't like the word 'survivor' but there aren't many others to use. Victim is the worst of all.

To survive is, according to the OED, from Anglo-Norman survivre, from Latin supervivere. Verb transitive: continue to live or exist after; outlive, outlast; remain alive or well in spite of (a danger, accident etc). Verb intransitive: continue to live or exist after some event (expressed or implied); be still alive or existent. Survival: the state or fact of continuing to live or exist after the cessation of something else.

For me, survival is about changing and growing. It's about uncovering and bringing things out of hiding. Survival is about being seen, staying in or near the light so the shadows don't overwhelm me.

Numbness. Numb: deprived of feeling or the power of movement, especially through extreme cold; incapable of sensation resulting from or characteristic of such deprivation. Numb: what you sometimes have to be in order to survive.

* * *

THE WORLD ACCORDING TO MY FATHER
16. SEX
(See *Love*)

* * *

28 September, 2009
I was passing near Ridgeway yesterday afternoon and decided at the last minute to drop in, but rang Annabel first. She said, *He's been asleep since midnight – fifteen hours already.*

I went straight up to his room. He was fast asleep on his back, hands together over the covers as though he'd fallen asleep praying. The colour and stillness of his head were like a wax effigy at Madame Tussauds. I didn't want him to wake. Ever.

I listened to his breathing for a few minutes, and left again.

* * *

Ciné film, 1953
The swing hangs from a large horizontal branch of a parkland tree. It could be a beech, possibly even an oak. The young woman half-sits on the swing seat, takes a few steps backwards and leans back, throwing her weight into the purpose of getting the swing moving. Soon she's swinging to and fro. Higher and higher. Each time she swings towards the camera, she beams, a sweet girlish smile, and tilts her head. Her wavy auburn hair

167

spreads gently away from her face as she moves through the
air.

* * *

I see my mother every day, even now.

She's there in my first waking moments and sometimes I have to shoo her away as I emerge from sleep – it's a time I want to be on my own and she doesn't seem to realise that. I like to open gently into half-light, hear the pigeons at the top of the chimneys and taste the day.

She stands by my bed, hushed, but I can feel her there. I know she wants me to wake. She relies on me to wake.

The first time I remember waking like this, aware of her by the bed, I was small enough to fit my head and shoulders into the pink fur fabric pyjama case that lived under my pillow. She had given it to me for Christmas the year before, when I was five and a half. I pulled the furry thing on tightly and tiny sparks snicked in the air around my face. I did up the zip as far as I could until it bit the skin on my chest. Then I buried my pink head between the pillow and the bottom sheet. It was hard to breathe, too hot to stay there long, and I could hear my mother's muffled laughter, so I came out, tugged off the pyjama case and threw it at her, tears burning in my eyes.

I used to think about doing it to her, to get my own back. If I woke in the middle of the night, I would sometimes tiptoe along the creaky passage, past the closed doors of my brothers' rooms, past the shadows of bookcases and potted plants. Past dark portrait faces of stern ancestors on the walls. I was going to wake my mother and stand by her and stare. I was going to make her feel like I felt.

Occasionally I heard no breathing at all from the other side of the door and I was filled with a morbid sense that my parents had both died in their sleep. More often though, the breathing sounds were long and slow and regular, with snoring from my father, occasional animal snuffles from my mother, the rhythm of their sleeping bodies comforting and mysterious. They left the door a few inches open so, if I wanted to go in, I just had to push it and there they were, laid out before me like two stone figures in a church.

But while I often went in to look, I never woke my mother. I would make the long-short journey to her side of the bed, the side nearest the door. I leaned over her and studied the place where her hair met her forehead, where the skin was soft and thin. I didn't need to stroke it because I knew how it felt. I thought of whispering in her ear, *Listen, it's me*, but I never did. I couldn't bear to disturb the stillness of her face, her lips a quiet line sealing in the words.

My father never stirred. His rest was of a different kind. It was as though he had gone into hibernation. He was far away. In sleep his features set into a serious mask, not unkind so much as featureless, quite different from the way my mother became more beautiful, more purely herself when she was asleep.

For my father, night was a way of getting ready for the next day. He slept on the far side, closer to the window. *So I only have to take four steps in the morning to see the garden*, he said when I asked him. He loved that morning view, though it made him anxious. He would gaze in silence for a few moments, then mutter about the length of the grass, even if there was no one listening to him. Even if it had just been cut. Next, more silence, except for the grunts that accompanied his floor stretches and press-ups. When he'd completed twenty of each, he pulled on his knee supports, laced up his running shoes and set off to cover three miles through the woods and around the fields, winter spring summer and autumn, whatever the weather.

After his shower he was transformed – dark city suit, striped shirt, cufflinks, ironed handkerchief, a pile of change counted from the chest of drawers into his trouser pocket. Often a red tie, and always the rolled-gold tie clip my mother had given him.

She was downstairs in the kitchen by now, preparing two poached eggs, timed precisely to be on the buttered toast, on the plate, on the table, for his arrival there. While she made the coffee, he polished his black shoes, placed two sets of keys by his briefcase. He left the house on the dot of seven.

* * *

THE WORLD ACCORDING TO MY FATHER
17. SLEEP

Sleep is a bank you pay into each night.

You are lucky if you sleep well.

If you don't sleep well, you need something to help you sleep.

Someone might ask you, *Are you asleep?* And you might answer, *No*. You cannot answer, *Yes*, and be telling the truth.

* * *

6 October, 2009

Yesterday was Dad's eighty-sixth birthday. He's at his favourite hotel in Devon with Annabel and Sue, the second carer. It's amazing that they were able to get him down there by car, as ill as he is. He's celebrating by eating and drinking. No matter that he's doubly incontinent.

I'm tempted to admire the sheer determination. He copes, according to Annabel, by dissociating himself from the mess and the smell and every other aspect of his body.

Sometimes I think he might live forever.

Annabel says he alternates between telling her he loves her and telling her he hates her.

7 October, 2009

Last night in the dining room at the hotel, after drinking three double whiskies and two bottles of wine, and while waiting for the pudding, he apparently asked the waiter for a bowl to vomit into. The man brought it and my father told him where to place it. In the end he didn't use it. He left the restaurant in his wheelchair, with the vomit bowl on his lap.

Sometimes the feelings that well up in me are beyond what I can articulate. The lump in my throat paralyses my mind. I feel sick myself. I don't know how to go on being associated with him in any sense. How can I cut myself away? The surgery is urgent yet I've waited a long time for this operation.

Today he's out of it, hardly responds, can't be woken, so Annabel and Sue have had to extend the stay at the hotel.

I long for release.

9 October, 2009

They're home again from Devon.

For a while, I felt him swing beyond the cliff, taking parts of me with him to hang over the edge. He was grappling with his angel – with his life, his death. He might have let go, could have let go at any moment. But he didn't. He's not yet ready to die. He has come back and is sitting again on the rocky ledge.

His voice is stronger and he's in less pain. In the course of a day, he can be truculent, irritable, spoiling for a fight, overly solicitous, possessive, critical, mistrustful. And just plain angry. Anger – the source of all his vigour.

Yesterday he threw up after a meal, a common occurrence, and when Annabel had cleaned him up, he told her that he enjoyed vomiting. He liked that sensation of emptying out. Has he found out that purging himself brings its own pleasure?

12 October, 2009

The night before last, in a dream, I was searching frantically in the bedclothes for some part of me, a lost body part. I couldn't find it. Then I realised I was looking for my face.

On the phone today, Dad told me he had just got back from Fort William. *A place you know well,* he said. Actually I've never been there, but my eldest brother Christopher worked near Fort William for a while.

Dad asked me, *Are you dead?*

No, I said, *I'm not dead.*

He seemed surprised.

Annabel feels that his end may be imminent. He's sinking into comatose states more often and for longer. Each time he comes back it seems his life is less secure. I'm letting go of him more and more, or trying to.

I still fear that I won't survive his death. That somehow he'll take me with him.

* * *

Ciné film, 1960
The woman is sitting on a garden chair against a brick wall, rocking a well-swaddled baby in her arms while three older children play. The camera at first attempts to cover both scenes, but as the older children demand more of the photographer's attention, the mother and child are abandoned and the camera slides away to focus on two boys who are chasing the girl across the lawn. The younger boy disappears and when he comes back into the action, he has a coat which he tosses over the girl's head as she moves between her brothers. She throws off her covering several times, but the boys replace it.

* * *

So many hours spent looking at the films. Between the DVD player and my laptop, I've now watched them many times, at different speeds and in various orders.

This morning I had the two DVDs running simultaneously. I sat on the sofa and flipped my gaze between them. I could freeze-frame the earlier films, halting the younger girl from time to time, whilst watching the older girl develop year on year.

I suppose my father had more time to use the ciné camera

on holiday and he liked capturing his family at play: swimming, digging on the beach, picnicking, rock-climbing. These beach holidays, mostly near Daymer Bay in Cornwall, alternate with skiing. Between the holidays, my father films the garden at Broomfields or Manor Farm, scanning the apple blossom and massed tulips and narcissi, the azaleas and rhododendrons, for some truth he hasn't found in the Swiss Alps or on the beaches facing out to the North Atlantic.

His version of our family life, the version we are left with, has us all together only two or three times a year. There are no weekends or evenings in our lives, and very few interiors. There is mostly a well-organised and active outdoor life, with barely a hint of the dull days, the arguments, the tantrums, the spilt drinks, the fights. The cruelty and the punishments. The black water beneath the beautiful white frozen surface.

My five and six-year-old self is free and natural, exactly how I would like to remember my childhood. I appear in a score of different swimsuits, shorts and T-shirts, my long fine hair escaping from clips and bands. I am frequently seen holding or brushing the blonde wisps back from my face while trying to do something else with the other hand – push a pram, dig a moat, pull the dog's tail. Occasionally an adult appears and ties my hair back. It always breaks away again.

I'm seldom still. I hop and spin, beam and gesture, my arms always active and hands expressive. I dance with my whole body. My face is light and smiley. I feature large in my father's casting and I'm naturally aware of my role in that way pretty young children are. *Why shouldn't I be centre stage? It's my place to be.*

Then there's the shift between one DVD and the next. At the end of the first, I'm on the beach in Cornwall. It must be Daymer

Bay, probably summer 1962. I'm wearing the pink polka-dotted swimsuit.

The second disk begins with swimming pool scenes at Manor Farm, just over a year later. Several of us children are messing around with rubber rings, racing one another and diving. We're all in the nude. I'm plump, my hair cropped short, and there is something about my demeanour that's altogether changed.

There's something different too in the way my father films me. The camera used to linger on me and I had a way of being in front of the lens that was natural and unaffected. From 1963 onwards, I look away or freeze when the ciné camera turns to me, standing still and showing that awareness of self that usually marks an older child, a pubescent child. Or else I perform to camera, deliberately climbing a rock and posing on its summit. Sequence after sequence shows these two behaviours, the girl either shying away from the camera or briefly meeting it with a self-conscious performance.

I feature less and less as the films go on. Where I do appear, I'm a serious, purposeful child, generally intent on some activity. In this child I see more easily the person I recognise as myself, the person that grew into the adult. Frequently my father pans over me and comes to rest on my younger brother.

There are just one or two sequences where I seem moody or unhappy. One in particular seems significant. I think my father is filming the start of a holiday.

* * *

Ciné film, 1964
Part of a river cruiser, its narrow decks. Two boys in jeans and
sweaters are first tying ropes, then larking about, pulling faces,

mouthing silent comments at the camera. The older boy shakes a boat-hook at the younger one. The woman is seated in the bow where there are recessed wooden benches. She gets to her feet, waves to camera. It looks like she is giving orders to the two boys. The girl is sitting opposite the woman, reading a book. The camera moves from the woman and stays on the reading girl for about ten seconds, until she looks up briefly, and immediately turns her head away. Red light intrudes from the sides of the shot. The picture dissolves and reforms into a faint image of two dinghies on the river.

* * *

Of course I wonder what's been edited out. I wonder which kinds of footage he rejected. I wonder if there's less footage of me, just as there's less of Christopher, as we get older, because we're the two who might give the lie to the happy-family fiction he wants to create. Our pictures might tell another story.

I could go on searching for evidence, reading what is and isn't there, except that the films are at risk of becoming something else to me after all this repeated viewing. Instead of being raw material for the story, they're becoming the story. I rewind and replay them, putting the clues into their own narrative, falling prey to the deadly logic of my father's editing, the seductive power of his will.

And I don't want it to be like this. I don't want it to be just a gathering of the fragments he has saved. I want the collection to be recognisably mine.

Modern technology seems to play tricks with my father's ordering, and from time to time different chapters of the DVDs are suppressed and then pop up again, interjecting a scene I had forgotten. Just like the way memory works.

Ciné film, 1962-3
Heavy falls of snow, laden trees, a half-built snowman with eyes and a pipe sticking out of a round mouth. Cut to daffodils and expanses of lawn...

Manor Farm, that first spring. I watch with a heavy feeling in my stomach, preparing to meet my new self – the girl with short hair and a cautious gaze.

The garden front of Broomfields, the second house in Dartford, the summer before the move to Sussex. A family group in which children and cousins, uncle and aunt, the woman and her mother, are all lined up next to garish flowerbeds.

I am brought almost to tears. There I am – still open-faced and luminous, hair down to my shoulders, six years old again.

* * *

THE WORLD ACCORDING TO MY FATHER
18. LOVE
(See *Sex*)

* * *

13 October, 2009

Before he dies, I'd like my father to show me ciné-film footage of the cliff hideaway, moving images of us both sitting there, shoulders propped together, looking out to sea.

I'd be eight years old but my hair would still be long. I'd be wearing shorts and plimsolls and my favourite blue-and-white polo shirt with a small red anchor embroidered on the left upper chest.

My father would speak into my ear and you would see his lips move. He would tell me I'd always be safe with him. He would promise to be the kind of parent he'd wanted for himself. He would pledge to try and understand me in ways his own father had never understood him. Those moments would be captured on film.

I'd like to have this instead of my imagined snapshot – a bent and ragged image, torn at the edges and scuffed across the middle, difficult to read and too imperfect to frame. There are two figures but they're sitting several feet apart, the faces unidentifiable, the colours distorted and faded.

* * *

In 1966, in the summer holidays following my eleventh birthday, my mother took me to Dickins & Jones in London to be fitted out with the bottle-green uniform for Ancaster House, a minor girls' public school.

The scrapbook records that she's found a boarding school to take me at eleven rather than thirteen which is more usual. She's heard that Ancaster House seems reasonable, and it isn't too far from Manor Farm. There's some urgency in her scrapbook entries around this time. She admits that she'll miss me dreadfully but consoles herself that I am *quite excited by the challenge of a boarding school*. For my part, I had seen my two elder brothers obliged to take this direction much earlier and so I regarded boarding school as a necessary adventure, an extension of the day-school world where I was already good at learning and knew how to please people.

I think my mother was protecting me, protecting everyone, by sending me away. I think this partly because I want to think it. She must have known, on some level, what was happening. Mustn't she? Perhaps she thought boarding school would break the pattern, or perhaps she was simply buying time. I wonder what else she could have done other than find ways of getting me away from home for long periods. She was thoroughly compromised by having four children and needing to stay with my father, her fifth child, who provided for us all. She was doing her best for me, her best for all of us. This is what I believe, at the moment.

At any rate, my first term at Ancaster House coincided with a change in my father. I was moved out of my first bedroom at Manor Farm to another room that was further from my parents' bedroom. I liked the new space, which was larger and lighter than my first room. I can't recall him abusing me in the old ways after that, though for years and years he would slap or pinch my bottom, and he often commented on the length of my skirt or how tight my jeans were. But, after that summer of 1966, I can't remember anything like the terrible abusive incidents of my early childhood. And I can recall more details of both my home life and my school life from that autumn onwards. There are fewer dust-sheeted rooms. I wonder if his stepmother's death earlier that same year also had a bearing on my father's changed behaviour?

I remember being homesick at boarding school, as so many others were. Ancaster House was not a kind institution and, in line with most other boarding schools in those days, the rules forbade contact between children and parents for the first few weeks. Even after that, opportunities for home visits were limited to two or three per term. On a Sunday out, there were a few glorious hours of emotional sunshine, but from lunchtime onwards, as the hands of the clock moved towards five o'clock and the inevitable trip back to school, the world became black and full of foreboding.

The separation from my home and my mother was a brutal shock. I wrote to her every day during the first year, begging her to find a way of making my life easier. *I am terribly homesick but I am trying to stick it for your sake. Please help me mummy… I miss you so much. I cry all the time… I could easily get out and run away only I dare not… I feel much worse in free time when my mind is not occupied with work. You have got to do something about it.* I drew sustenance from the regular letters my mother wrote back, and from the love that she and I had weighed into four-ounce bags of pink-and-white marshmallows, later doled out by Matron at the rate of one bag per week.

Despite my unhappiness, which eased to some extent after the first year, I continued to do well academically. My habit of using work as anaesthetic and cure-all was already well established, and the reports throughout my time at Ancaster House are positive about my progress. The same adjectives keep coming up: *careful, reliable, sensible, conscientious, determined, quiet, precise, orderly, polite.*

My mother's entry in the scrapbook for September 1967 admits that the first year at Ancaster House has been *a big disappointment.* She outlines the difficult process of deciding to look for another school. She agonises about moving me, fearing that the disruption might be as damaging as keeping me at the unhappy school which is at least familiar. In the end, we take the decision together, and in May 1968 I start at Benenden where I settle and begin to make new friends.

There's an overwhelming air of relief in my mother's scrapbook entry for September 1968. *We cannot speak too highly of the welcome Clare got at Benenden. The place is bright, cheerful, and as unoppressive as Ancaster House was oppressive. Clare has blossomed.*

Here, half way down the page of 1968, my mother's writing in the scrapbook ends. I am thirteen and happier than I have been in many years. My mother is content to close the book and get on with other things.

* * *

15 October, 2009
Philip and Freddie and I will go over to Dad's on Sunday. My youngest brother, Philip, will take his two boys aged thirteen and eleven, and his girl of nine. The idea is to get the children together and let off some fireworks. A sort of belated celebration of Dad's birthday.

* * *

That Sunday, when we arrive at my father's house, he's slouched in his big armchair, surrounded by my brother's family.

I sit down on the sofa to Dad's left, close to his better ear.

He looks across at my niece and tells her, *You're a sweetie.* Then he asks her, *Do you know what men do with sweeties?*

She doesn't answer.

They eat them, one of her brothers volunteers.

My father starts to say something else, but stops again. There's an awkward silence, then…

I can hardly believe what I'm witnessing. Adrenalin floods my bloodstream. Fight, flight, or freeze. With him, I always freeze.

I feel his bony left hand settle on my knee, crawl under my skirt, up my thigh. Simultaneously his right index finger moves to his lips. A theatrical gesture, blatant and flamboyant. *Ssshhhh.*

He stares deliberately at the children and the other adults present. Defiant.

He is two people at once. One is doing what he knows is wrong. The other is daring us to speak even as he tells us not to.

When at last I am able to move, I take his left hand out from under my skirt and put it carefully back in his lap. As I do so, his right hand leaves his lips and smacks his left hand. He smiles at me. That face I know so well – wily and sly, the eyes penetrating, all-seeing.

It seems that in the end he could not resist this last performance. *This is who and what I am. I know it and so do you.* There's none of the self-loathing and remorse I've hoped he'd show. There's no explanation. No apology to me. No tears. There's simply this final and very public acting out of what he has always been.

Later the same evening, when Annabel has helped my father to bed, brushed his teeth and settled him for the night, I go upstairs. I push his door open and step into the room. Just far enough. Standing in semi-darkness, looking down on the slight shape of him beneath the bedclothes, I can at last imagine him dead. But not yet. Not quite yet.

He turns his head in my direction. *Is that you?*

I've come to say goodnight. I'm leaving now.

I don't know who he thinks I am. I've no wish to make sure he knows it's me. I have nothing more to say to him. I'm still frozen in that moment of the ending to our long relationship. I know that something is complete. Not in the way I'd hoped for, but complete nonetheless because I've decided to end it at last.

Without speaking, he turns his head so it is in line with the pole of his body.

His skull is becoming a *memento mori*, a sculptural hollowed-out thing on a black velvet cushion, divorced from the rest of the bones.

I take my leave, closing the door behind me on the night room and the slightly rasping breath.

* * *

23 October, 2009

I won't see Dad again. Or anyway not for at least a month or six weeks. If at the end of that time he's still alive and I feel differently, I might allow myself to think about it, might review it. And if I don't, I won't.

I've said goodbye, in many ways. I've done my duty and what was never my duty and what became my duty. I've done much too much. For too many long years. When he leaves, it will be without my hand to hold, without what comfort I bring. When he dies, he'll go alone into the next, whatever that is for him. That's how it should be, and must be.

Over these few days I've reached a place at the bottom of tears. I've begun to grieve, in a sudden mighty release, the father he never was and the father he has been. And my own childhood.

I've been to my darkest and most cavernous sad places. And I've felt the fury working its way through me.

I can't yet think beyond these strange, tumbled, empty days. All I know is that Sunday was definitive. In one chilling moment he exposed his true self and in doing so broke the spell. I'm no longer his captive. He must die. And I will live.

He has a chest infection. The doctor has prescribed antibiotics but says Dad is unlikely to survive.

I've been thinking about snow falling, snow filling footprints in the snow, building layer upon layer of crystals until eventually the surface is even.

And of course, I've been thinking about the thaw. The black water. Everything that's revealed.

28 October, 2009
The doctor has told us to be ready for his death. Soon. Annabel has nursing support. She has what she needs.

I'll stay here, at home, and hold on tight. Try and get on with the business of living, doing the work I have to do as best I can. And cooking and keeping house for my family. Waiting.

* * *

In my imagination, I'm lying alone on a cliff ledge, on my stomach. The cliff is made of glass so when I look down it's as though I'm falling, or suspended mid-fall. The granite and lichens and stunted grasses cling to the glass cliff, making a micro landscape. By studying its detail, I can be engrossed. I can read where I am. It's only if I turn over and lie on my back that I feel vertigo, and that's because of the way the sky moves, too fast, unpredictable and wild. So I will stay on my front, looking down, the landscape holding me on my narrow glass ledge. This is my place: secure, transparent, terrifying.

Meanwhile my father lies in his bed, under sheets and blankets, on a protected mattress, his body spouting urine and faeces and vomit and pus and sweat like a poisoned many-headed hydra.

Annabel wakes him periodically to give him antibiotics and sips of water, to clean him up and make him comfortable enough to slip back into sleep. Apparently when he can form words he calls, *Mummy*. When his pain peaks he draws his knees to his chest and cries out, telling her how cruel she is, how she doesn't look after him and lets him suffer. He says he can bear it no longer.

All his suffering, all of it, expressed in one word. *Mummy*. A longing for home, for mother.

* * *

29 October, 2009

All day spent waiting. All of us, waiting, in our different places.

Regular phone calls with Annabel. Dad is alternately lucid and deeply asleep. Occasionally he speaks a few words in French. He takes small amounts of juice and water by syringe into his mouth. He says he's going to recover. He doesn't want to be alone.

Late morning, Annabel tells me his chest sounds very bad. At noon the nurses wash him and wet shave him and he seems to enjoy that. They move him into the centre of his big bed, for safety.

At tea time, the District Nurse gives him an injection of diamorphine.

Evening: his breathing is shallow and rapid.

Later, towards midnight, the breathing is shallow but even. There's a bubbling sound from his upper chest. He surfaces briefly, says he's going to get better. His forehead burns.

* * *

In my dream he's sitting on a little girl's bed. My bed. The girl begs for one of his bedtime stories about Fifi.

Fifi is his own invention, a beautiful blonde-haired woman with a flashing green eye and a flashing red one. She has a hollow wooden leg in which she keeps all number of secret things. When she's in trouble, she unscrews her leg to find what she needs.

Tonight the story goes like this. Fifi meets a sailor in a dark alley. She doesn't like the look of him so she tells him to go ahead and wait for her around the corner. She quickly unscrews her leg, takes out a loaded revolver and goes to find the sailor. She shoots him in the neck, replaces the revolver in her wooden leg, and hobbles home.

* * *

I wake soon after four. I've had four hours sleep. Enough.

At six I call Annabel. She says my father seems stronger and more comfortable this morning. He's talking and has taken some water. Annabel and Sue have changed his bed linen and propped him up on extra pillows to assist his breathing.

Around half past six I take a shower, try and prepare myself for whatever this day might bring. I practise breathing deeply. By seven I have to lie down, a cracking headache and I can't

186

move my legs. I take two paracetamol, and half an hour later two ibruprofen. The pain has shifted a little by eight, but I feel dreadful. As though I'm fading out. Dying.

Annabel calls me just after nine. My father's colour is better. She thinks he's coming through the infection.

I realise what's happening. In some way my father is drawing on my strength to keep a hold on his own life.

I know what I must do. I go downstairs and I sit cross-legged on the floor in front of the long window onto the garden. I close my eyes and ask to have my strength back. *I need my life. And he doesn't need me anymore,* I say repeatedly. And I add a last goodbye, before mentally I cut him free. I hold in my mind an image of a climber with an injured person dangling below on a rope. The climber cuts the rope.

I sit there, scarcely moving, for an hour.

The phone rings at ten forty. It's Annabel. I'm cooking breakfast for Freddie and his friend who's stayed over.

Your father has suddenly dipped. His pulse is weak.

I stand at the stove, prodding the bacon. My headache begins to recede.

Just before eleven, another call. Annabel can hardly form words. I wait, the phone pressed to my left ear, my eyes tight shut. I'm listening with every part of me.

At last she manages to say, *We can't find a pulse.*

It's a while before I understand that this means my father has died.

All I can feel is relief.

* * *

Thank you, my father, for taking me to Dartford paper mill on Saturday afternoons.

Thank you for lifting me up so I could peer into the bubbling vats of pulp.

Thank you for standing with me as I watched the paper rolling over the machines on huge hot cylinders.

Thank you for letting me take home sheets and sheets of it, all different colours.

There was always plenty of paper in our house, and I thank you for that.

* * *

26 November, 2009

One day soon it'll be time to finish writing about these things. My pen will meet its shadow in a full stop. It'll be time to close the book and set it aside. Very soon.

The memory of the morning of his death is already settling and taking its place in my own story. Nothing can be the same after that, the way nothing could be the same at the beginning of my life, after what he did – the way he made me his.

Goodbye to the phone calls I used to make, dreading my need to hear his voice grow more frail each time. Goodbye to how I would imagine him lying on his deathbed, the way I saw him that Sunday night, the last time. Goodbye to the final days, knowing and not knowing that he was about to die, feeling that strange earthward tug in my own guts, the pull of gravity. Goodbye.

Things are shifting back into place. His life, like a storm, has passed. The signs of meteorological disturbance are vanishing like some magician's trick. The sky must be clearing.

* * *

All through the weeks after his death, days of phone calls with family members, with the undertaker, choosing hymns and flowers and careful words for the funeral, days of writing letters and emails, all through these times I struggle to honour the best of my father in the rituals of his passing while allowing my private knowledge an equal but internal stature. By doing this, I can survive hearing what others write and say of him, can even begin to imagine the man they knew.

I want to be whole. I want to feel grief like a normal person but I know this can't be my way of grieving. Mine must be piecemeal, a little here and a little there. A memory of a shared meal. A walk together up a snowy path on Christmas morning. Tiny things. Mostly, a terrible, empty, quiet raging.

I strive to allow the other bits of the man in the same frame with the man I've feared and loathed, and like those crudely overlapping green-and-red images that become three-dimensional when you put on the special spectacles, he finally comes to life in the wake of his death, a fragile miracle of my own reconstruction. But always the images drift apart again. This is one of his legacies to me. Double vision. I can only remind myself that from time to time there is a third image, the living breathing spectre containing everything he was, the whole person.

* * *

Six Rendezvous with a Dead Man

The door from the foyer swings. A slice of brightness grows and shrinks, delivering them one by one to find their seats. The band's warming up, auditorium thick with sax, bass, keyboard, drums. I'm sinking into rhythm when I catch his rich sweet scent – that cologne he's always slapped around his neck and chin each morning and again each night. The knowledge of him trapped within my cells, all I can keep, alone in the dark.

He sits in the ladder-back chair, beside me. *Not carcinoma,* he snaps, t*hat was the secondary cause, the primary cause was pneumonia.* The Registrar staples papers, signs fifteen copies of the death certificate. Seals them in an envelope. She clears her throat, thanks me for the cheque, asks if there's anything else before I go. He darts me that sideways look, *Let's get the hell out of here. I need a drink.*

An hour to check two hundred service sheets. Him at my elbow, in his best dark suit, striking my knuckles with his metal rule each time the print is anything but monochrome. Copy by copy I discover magenta raked across lines of type, yellow and blue smearing the space between the second hymn and the Committal. Some copies are clean. He tells me to pile those neatly in a box marked *GOOD.*

I find the Bitter Aloes when I'm clearing shelves. The cap sheds crystals as I twist and pour the tincture onto my palm. Dip in the tip of my tongue. I'm six again, he's painting all my fingers and both thumbs. Later, in bed, I suck and suck until the gall inhabits my mouth. The juices do their work, purge my sins, seal my lips. Time goes on. He adds bitters to his nightly gin. I understand that I need punishing.

The swimming hour: down and back. All the years: down and back. No need to think of him, no need to look. Down and back: learning to forget. Perhaps he never lived. Stretch, kick, breathe; under, up and breathe. Down and back. Vision alternating between silent fluid world and air above. Then I see him. Standing at the deep end, by the clock, his right index finger beckoning. That way he has.

I wait in the cold for the people who take away stairlifts and deathbeds, the paraphernalia of a long decline. Standing in room after room, I seek his absence, as if the print of him here is the proof I want. He's gone. Not for me the desire to touch his clothing or pull the hair from his comb. And when the bedroom door closes on its own, I welcome his invisibility, the mystery that's parted his matter from mine.

* * *

I arrive at Ridgeway late, well after dark on a Sunday night in December. I have to tap numbers into the keypad to gain entry for my car through the gates. The code is the year of my father's marriage to my mother, 1947. The gates buzz and swing inwards.

There at the top of the drive is the skip we filled last weekend. It has rained every day since then so that the contents have formed a thick aromatic soup, a bouillabaisse of my father's life remnants – newspapers and catalogues, ancient pots of herbs and packets of pasta from the store cupboard, half-used cosmetics, old pillows, wire coathangers, incontinence pads and catheter tubes the district nurses wouldn't take back. And all the rest.

I've come and gone several times since he died. On those visits the house still felt like his home and wore a variety of guises – the funeral, the family weekend of junk clearing. There were lights, cars, activity.

This is different. Letting myself in tonight is like breaking and entering.

The house is cold. I fumble for the light switch. There are items I see as though for the first time. Was this chair always green? Did that picture hang there on my last visit? Where did the pack of cards come from?

I leaf through the stack of post. I check all the windows. I walk into every room, looking for something. Not him, I tell myself as I tour the house. But actually I'm not so sure.

Now to the real purpose of my visit. I go back to the corner of the sitting room where his big armchair is plumped with cushions and I unplug the TV, gathering up the leads and instruction booklets, the remote controls. I load them into the back of my car, leaving and re-entering by the front door with the security lights flicking on and off, illuminating my felony in a series of monochrome stills.

My father loved his television. He spent long hours of his final months sitting in front of it, enchanted by the bright colours, the action and the noise. This TV was his true companion. He preferred it to the carers or the visitors who came. And now, because our old TV has broken, and my brothers don't want this one, it's to be mine – this giant box of moving images, emitter of truth, means of escape, source of illusion.

* * *

14 December, 2009
I've finally had a conversation with Lucia about what Dad told her all those months ago. We spoke on the phone. I said I had to know more. There were long pauses. She was a reluctant witness.

Even now I find it very hard to tell you.

Please try, I said. *It will make a difference to me.*

That night he was quite distraught. He seemed to need to talk about things he had to face up to before he died. The drink had relaxed him. He wanted to talk to me, but what I noticed, well, when he started about you, it was as though he was two people... He was struggling with himself.

Go on, I urged.

One minute he was saying, 'I don't know why Heather didn't say anything, she always knew everything. She should have told me...'

I waited for what might come next. Nothing.

And what else did he say?

He said, 'It must have been me... It was me. I thought it was normal, I thought it was what fathers do.'

I had the feeling something was over. She was not going to say more. The silence was the kind that sounds as though the line has gone dead.

Finally she said, *That's really all. It made me feel terrible to hear it. I didn't want to hear it.*

Thank you, I said.

We went on talking for a few moments. I can't think what it was about. Small talk. We said goodbye.

After I'd put the phone down, I stayed sitting at my desk. Then the tears came.

19 December, 2009

Last night I dreamed of him. He came back from somewhere else, a nursing home, hospital, death? He came back to throw an elaborate formal party in the empty house that had been his.

He was behaving as I'd experienced him throughout his last years. He was demanding, difficult, and busy spending a great deal of money to make the place exactly as he wanted it with fresh paint, new light fittings, and furniture bought especially for the occasion. There he was in his tatty old tracksuit, in charge of the house makeover, issuing orders whilst people painted walls, delivered wine and fitted curtains.

He insisted that all children would have to be locked up in a room well away from the adults so they didn't disturb the party.

Nothing was ready on time. Dad's idea of hell. The guests started arriving in evening dress at the front of the house while people were running around positioning items of furniture, hanging pictures, putting cocktail sausages and prawns onto plates. Electricians were still wiring up a set of crystal chandeliers.

I was aware of all this from upstairs. I was locked in the children's room.

* * *

Sorting out my father's belongings, more than a year after his death, I find a slim, cloth-bound book, sea-green in colour, about six inches by nine inches, entitled 'The Progress Book: An Illustrated Register of Development from Birth till Coming of Age and After'.

I've never seen it before. I never knew of its existence.

The introduction to the book stresses the importance of keeping records of Children's Ailments, External Peculiarities and Hereditary Peculiarities.

On the page headed Birth Records, my grandfather has written details of his youngest son's birth at *1, Alipore Park, Calcutta, on 5th October 1923, 12.30 am, Weight 6 lbs 4 oz, Eyes blue, Hair light brown.*

At the foot of this page, beneath the sub-heading Special Facts, three poignant sentences: *His mother's illness started soon after his birth. Had her troubles been correctly diagnosed from the start she might have been spared years of misery. The best doctors in Tropical Medicine did not recognise it until it had got to too advanced a stage.*

My father's mother suffered from tropical sprue for more than five years. The cause of this disease is inflammation of the small intestine due to excess levels of certain bacteria. Food can't be absorbed. Symptoms include abdominal cramps, chronic diarrhoea, anaemia, weight loss, anorexia, and eventually organ failure. My father's mother died in London in March 1929. Even in the 1920s, the disease was curable if diagnosed in time.

The Progress Book has a Baptismal Register. It records that my father was baptised at St Paul's Cathedral, Calcutta, on the first of December 1923. Then there are pages for each year, headed Progress End of First Year, Progress End of Second Year and so on. On each of these pages, up to the Sixth Year, my father's father has recorded brief details of his youngest child's life, and has mounted photographs. The annual records stop abruptly the year my father's mother died, although some short notes have been added later, on other pages, even as late as 1939.

The rest of the book consists of graphs for Weight Gain; pages for Development of Teeth, Medical History and Mental Progress; pages for Educational Records and Religious Progress, for Recreations and Amusements, Holiday Records and Interesting Events; even pages for Finger Prints. Most of these pages are blank.

Finding The Progress Book is a gift. The intimate entries in my grandfather's neat script cast new light on my father's early life. The most striking realisation is the paternal care and love evident from my grandfather's words. This stern middle-aged man, known in the family as The Last Victorian, writes so tenderly of his youngest son. Yet this is the man of whom my father said, opening his own oral memoir, *I've always been a bit puzzled why we never really got to grips with each other. The relationship was really rather attenuated and difficult.*

Later, my father said that his father never visited him at school or took any interest in him. When his father died in 1943, my father did not attend the funeral.

Soon after his mother died and his stepmother arrived on the scene, my father was sent away to boarding school. His emotional development from the age of six, and his navigation of the stormy waters of adolescence, were framed by the conditions of prep-school and public-school life in the England of the 1930s. His finishing school, from 1941, was the lower deck of His Majesty's Royal Navy. I'll only ever know the bare facts from those years.

I'm not excusing my father's despicable behaviour, I'm not even attempting to explain it. I'm just setting down some points that may or may not have a bearing on how life shaped him.

Once upon a time there was a little boy who was *of a particularly affectionate nature, with very attractive ways, resulting in great popularity,* whose father indulged his love of riding on the top deck of a London bus, *perfect heaven,* took him to the Lord Mayor's Show and taught him the names of all the stops on the Central Line. A little boy whose *adoration of his elder brothers was very marked* and who had *such a vivid imagination that he could make a good game with very simple ingredients.*

* * *

Ciné film, 7th birthday, 1962
The game of Pass the Parcel is finished. The children have balloons now. They bounce them, chase them and squeeze them until they burst. In their midst, the girl, in her white satin-and-net party dress with a blue sash, pats a red balloon upwards into the air, and dances around underneath it.

* * *

September, 2011
It's almost two years since my father died in his last house, the tenth home since he married my mother in 1947.

He loved Ridgeway with its steep drop to beech woods and long views towards the silhouette of the South Downs. The house was a consolation after my mother went to the care home and soon became a symbol of my father's renaissance. He was proud that he'd chosen the place himself, extended it as he wished and decorated it according to his own taste.

We're in the process of selling this house. The long farewells of sorting out, packing up, distributing his chattels, the last of my mother's chattels, these are nearly done.

During my most recent and possibly last visit, I came across the book of Robert Frost poems I'd given Dad after discovering he liked 'Stopping by Woods on a Snowy Evening'. I put it in my bag. And later that day, at the back of a cupboard in my father's kitchen, I found my mother's tin box of recipe cards with her favourite cakes and casseroles neatly described. I brought that home too. Another of her boxes, to go with the leather jewellery case.

If all goes according to plan, the remaining physical traces of my father will be cleared from his house in a few weeks' time. And where will he be then, when this particular agglomeration of things and scents and colours – this essence of him – is no longer contained and configured within the building where he lately lived?

He'll be in the garden where he heard of his mother's death, and in the Mediterranean ports of his wartime youth. He'll be in the waves of the English Channel. In the falling snow. And he'll be in these words, written by someone who is at last happy and fulfilled, deeply loved and loving, blessed in so many ways. A person who laughs and cries and lives her life.

Afterword

It was difficult to start writing this book but in some ways it's even more difficult to finish it. This is because I've been living and reliving it, writing and rewriting it all my life. At every stage I've continued to uncover the story and craft it into something that's better and clearer and closer to my truth.

It is good to let go now, but I'm losing a companion. That feeling comes with the completion of any project or book – it's particularly acute in this case because the work is so personal. It is central to who I am.

My relationship with the past goes on evolving. Since 2011, where the book ends, I've at times needed to write more. These extra pieces are grouped together here. The first, the List of Charges, has made me feel so intensely uncomfortable, and so unwilling to cause discomfort in others, that I almost decided to exclude it. In the end I'm including it precisely because of the discomfort. This is what needs to be stated clearly, although some days it is more difficult than others.

* * *

A List of Charges Against My Father

My father took a sexual interest in my buttocks and vagina when I was a small child. He often touched these parts of my body. I can't remember when it started.

My father put his penis in my mouth until he ejaculated. He did this from 1963 when I was seven.

My father put his fingers inside my vagina when I was seven or eight. This happened a number of times.

My father played cruel games, forcing me to touch my vagina and other parts of my body at his command. He did this on several occasions. I can't remember how many.

For a while my father used to come into my bedroom in the night. I can remember waking up when he touched me under the bedclothes. Sometimes I tried to pretend I hadn't woken.

My father forced physical contact I did not want.

My father pinched and slapped my bottom and made sexually-suggestive remarks throughout my childhood and adolescence and into my adult life.

I do not know if my father ever had full intercourse with me. Some memories are blocked off and I doubt if I will ever know.

My father told me he loved me and we shared a secret that was just for us.

My father made me promise not to tell anyone what he did to me.

My father constantly made sexual remarks about my body and about the clothes I was wearing, from my early childhood until his death in 2009 when I was fifty-four.

My father criticised me and humiliated me frequently, often in front of other people.

My father took an inappropriate interest in my relationships with all the male friends I brought home.

My father swore at me and cursed me.

My father told lies about me.

My father did many other things which I am not ready to detail.

My father never acknowledged any of it. He never apologised.

* * *

My father was emotionally neglected as a child. His mother died when he was five. He went to boarding school at the age of six. He might have had a sexual relationship with his stepmother in his teens. He was probably raped when he joined the lower deck of the Royal Navy at age seventeen. All his life he was obsessed by sex and obeyed his sexual impulses, even when they were damaging and directed towards his own daughter. He betrayed the trust placed in him and instead of facing up to it, he had another gin or another whisky.

As a child I was in thrall to my father and for decades I wasn't able to perceive or accept the full extent of the problems he'd caused. It's difficult to describe this. Many people don't understand the power of a profoundly-abusive relationship. The abused, the target, is emotionally, mentally and often materially captive, and this captivity can last well beyond the period of the worst abuse, particularly if the abuser is a family member and if, as in my case, the target has been conditioned to abuse since early childhood. The entire family suffers, of course, because there's something very sick in its midst. Any potential or actual revelations of abuse threaten what stability there is – another reason that the truth often remains buried. Usually the family will fragment once the truth is declared. Sometimes it never comes together again.

* * *

People ask me, directly or indirectly, *Why did you continue to care for your father as you did? Why didn't you walk away?* He had such a strong hold over me that I would not have known how to walk away. I've never known a loving father; I only knew this father. At times, I believed that he did love me. At other times I felt he didn't love me but that I deserved the treatment he dished out to me. I wasn't sure what I felt for him. I had no yardstick for what I should feel. I thought I felt love and hate. I understand now that it was an attachment based almost entirely on fear. Over time I filled up with fear and shame.

Added to this, I had grown up with a strong sense of duty and daughterly obligation. Women of my generation were shaped by a world in which daughters took on caring roles, come what may. I had already been the caring mainstay to both my parents throughout their marriage and this continued, on and off, up to my mother's death in 1999. When my father became seriously ill, I was the person expected to respond to his calls for help, liaise with his GP, arrange for carers to come, and all the rest. There were assumptions within the family and among my father's friends and I was largely unable to resist them.

I suppose that I might have been forgiven for walking away if I'd dared to out my own truth while my father was living, but I wasn't at all ready to do so. Only his death gave me the freedom to fully realise my truth and then reveal it in public, and this process has had to happen slowly and gradually because of the great risks for my own mental and emotional health.

* * *

I think at last I know my anger, and I know how to say No and Yes.

The sporadic bouts of gut and back pain I've been having since Dad first became seriously ill have been, I'm convinced, the body's expression of him and of my feelings about him.

These pains, these expressions, have calmed down since his death.

Because of my symptoms, it's been suggested I undergo colonoscopy. I can be good at listening to medical advice, but I've said no. In saying no to a colonoscopy, I'm finally saying no to my father, which gives me a new sense of what my body is and where its boundaries are. The thought of a colonoscopy is associated with traumatic memories, and the prospect of sedation or anaesthesia ('you will be compliant' as one doctor put it) brings tension and fear. What state might I be in when I come round from such a procedure?

So if I've said the no I couldn't say as a child, what is it no to? It's no to my father, no to his desires, no to having my body invaded, to the loss of dignity, to sleeping or blanking while something is done to me. No to not knowing, to forgetting, to humiliation. To being talked down to, rubbished, devalued. No to being told what's good or not good for me, to being misunderstood. No to being compliant. No to not being heard. No to screaming in a vacuum. No to nightmares. No to my own need to repeat and repeat the wrong behaviours. No to victimhood and helplessness. No to being raped, to having things taken from me, to being hoodwinked. No to anyone who breaches my privacy and my space. No to being mind-fucked. No to anything I don't want. No.

And if I have now said no, loudly and forcibly, let me think about the ways in which I can say yes.

I say yes to being my own boss, yes to my body as I say it shall be, yes to being in charge of myself. Yes to love and compassion. Yes to the child me; I will do for her now what she could not do for herself back then. Yes to letting her grow. Yes to telling other people about my experiences. Yes to publication, yes to being able to contribute to the public debate about all these things. A great big resounding yes to being heard. Yes to all good people who have the right ideas and feelings. Yes to all good men. Yes to change. Yes to peace. Yes to my own creativity for ever and ever, to meeting my dreams. Yes to the next stage, to all the other books I want to write. Yes to life, yes to whatever it brings, yes to my voice and the resonance of it. Yes to goodbye Dad.

That last yes is the most important of all. I needed to think I could love him by giving him a chance to explain himself at the end of his life. I wanted to seek some sort of resolution. And I had to find a place to be with the conflicting feelings. I can be done with him now. I have entered a new phase in which he has no place. He is no longer inside me. I have expressed him and put him out.

Acknowledgements

I offer heartfelt thanks and appreciation to:

My fully functional 'writing family' of colleagues – writers, readers, commentators. You are exceptional.

Those who have worked with me therapeutically, particularly Mica who knows what this writing has meant.

Isobel Dixon and Hattie Grünewald at Blake Friedmann for their faith in me and in the book, and for their persistent support.

Lynn Michell for being the passionate and compassionate publisher this book needed. I have thoroughly enjoyed the collaboration with her and the Linen Press team.

Small indie presses everywhere for their dedication and daring.

Neil Gower for his vision, literally.

Philip for picking up the pieces so many times and handing them back to me, and for always being sure of the power of remaking.

Freddie for his astonishing love and understanding.

Short extracts from this book have previously been published in *True Tales from the Old Hill* (Frogmore Press, 2015) and on the University of Brighton website. My thanks to the editors.

References

Female Survivors of Sexual Abuse: an integrated guide to treatment (2002) by Christine D. Baker

The Invisible Epidemic: Post-Traumatic Stress Disorder, Memory and the Brain (2011) by J. Douglas Bremner

Chronic Self-Injury & Self-Mutilation in Adult Survivors of Incest and Childhood Sexual Abuse (1993) by David Calof

Understanding the Effects of Child Sexual Abuse (2009) by Sam Warner

The following organisations work with people who have experienced or been affected by abuse:

Childline; Mind; NAPAC; NSPCC; Rape Crisis England and Wales; Refuge; Safeline; Survivors UK; The Survivors Trust; The Truth Project

Lightning Source UK Ltd.
Milton Keynes UK
UKHW02f2204110818
327101UK00007B/423/P